Bong
Appétit

Bong Appétit

Mastering the Art of Cooking with Weed

Editors of **MUNCHIES**

with Elise McDonough
Photographs by Marcus Nilsson
Illustrations by Ho-Mui Wong

PAVILION

Contents

Recipe List

Introduction

People have been eating weed for thousands of years – brewed for tea, crumbled into coffee, as a tincture, mixed with fruits and spice in jam – but in the last decade or so, it has started to feel very different. Building on the accumulated wisdom of traditional recipes such as Middle Eastern *mahjoun* and Indian *bhang,* cannabis cuisine has gone far beyond brownies and has reclaimed its place as a serious culinary ingredient. We're now living in a new era of marijuana cuisine; one of space-age vaporisers, designer hash and cutting-edge science, all of which have helped take weed food to a whole other realm.

In these pages, we're experimenting with weed, but not like teenage stoners hitting a homemade gravity bong. Instead, we have enlisted some incredible chefs to make weed food that eclipses those early brownies – the kind of fare that you'd want to sit down and eat even if there wasn't weed in it.

Through a mash-up of modern cooking techniques and hard-won weed wisdom, television series *Bong Appétit* highlights next-level ingredients and techniques that are revolutionising the way we use cannabis, as a culinary ingredient – leafy green; spice; dried herb; refined, isolated chemical – and as something that gets you high.

Envied for its extensive pantry filled with fine flowers, rare hashes, infused oils and weed-infused spices, *Bong Appétit* (the show) redefines luxury in many respects. We realise that many readers, even those who live in places where recreational cannabis is legal, won't have access to these products. So we've translated many ideas from the series into something that works for the home cook. Do you have access to terpenes, cannabinoids, distillates, tinctures and any strain of bud you desire and are looking for new techniques that will put them on your home table or turn them into professional-level edibles? These recipes will give you plenty to work with. Do you have to text someone shady as hell to get hooked up, so you basically have to work with whatever you can get? There are recipes here for you, too.

And we're making it easy to know just how high you'll get from a plate of fried chicken wings (see page 166) or a bowl of pappardelle Bolognese (see page 149). We lab tested all of our recipes to make sure you wouldn't have to worry about (a) wasting a bunch of weed making food that doesn't get you high or (b) making food that gets you so high you have to call in sick for work the next day. We've also asked *Bong Appétit* hosts Vanessa Lavorato and Ry Prichard to add notes and pro tips throughout the book so you get perspective from seasoned experts.

And sure, there's some crazy shit in here, like poaching a whole octopus in weed olive oil or force-infusing THC into alcohol with a whipped-cream charger. But we're also keeping it simple enough for the beginner cook to play along, with cannabis getting into most of the recipes via easy-to-make infusions of butter or oil. Still, if you're itching for a challenge, you'll find plenty of next-level options, from cannabis-leaf kimchi to infused pepperoni.

Some of what you may have seen on the show flies in the face of the conventional wisdom that prioritises budget over flavour when cooking with weed. We freely admit that burning three ounces of high-quality pot in a smoker or dumping a handful of herb into a fryer was more about experimentation than getting high. You won't find recipes for that kind of thing here. That said, if you feel like going all out, we're not here to stop you. This book is all about giving you the tools and savvy you need to master the art of cooking with cannabis – no matter what that looks like for you.

If you live in a place without legal weed, please know we're sorry – and that you are not alone. And, yes, it's incredibly fucked up that there are millions of people in prison for enjoying the kind of recreational activity you're about to read an entire book on, and we're hoping that changes soon too. In any case, rest assured that the recipes in this book can be followed without including any cannabis at all. They're still excellent; they're just not quite as fun.

Equipment

Sadly, not everyone can live in cannabis-friendly Los Angeles with an elaborately outfitted pot pantry in their kitchen like on *Bong Appétit*. On the bright side, you don't need much more than your basic kitchen essentials to cook with weed. So in addition to the usual pots and pans, knives, spoons and bowls, here is what you will need.

Canning/preserving jars: Vital for using the jar method for infusing. The size you need depends on what you are infusing, so keep an array of different sizes in your cupboard, as well as back-up lids and bands. When used in boiling water, the lids and bands can degrade quickly and put your precious cannabis oils at risk of becoming waterlogged.

Muslin cloths: Essential for straining cannabis plant matter out of finished infusions.

Digital kitchen scales: Reliable measurements are especially important when dealing with cannabis flowers, kief and extracts to ensure correct dosing. Look for high-quality scales capable of precise measurements down to the milligram.

Instant-read thermometer: Cannabis infusions require attention to temperature throughout the process, making our instant-read thermometer the gift that keeps on getting us high.

Mesh strainers: Indispensable for creating infusions. Having mesh strainers on hand in a variety of sizes is a good idea as it will allow you to work at any scale.

Microplane grater: This fine-rasp grater is ideal for grating tiny bits of hash or flower over finished dishes. It is also especially helpful if you're working with compressed chunks of hash.

Rubber spatulas: For scraping every bit of THC-laced batter out of a bowl.

Once you have the basics on hand, you will want to think about some nice-to-have options.

Coffee grinder: If you're cooking with weed frequently, or need to grind up larger quantities of weed that would overload a simple herb grinder, a dedicated coffee grinder is very helpful.

Dab tools: If you anticipate doing a lot with cannabis extracts, you might want a set of dab tools – little spoons, pokers and angled sharp-edged implements – plus a bottle of isopropyl alcohol for getting your tools clean. 'Iso' can be bought in some high street chemists (but is easily found online if not) and has a number of household uses – grease remover, disinfectant, glass cleaner – precisely what you need to clean sticky dab tools as well as gunky glass pipes and dirty grinders. Buy tools sold as 'wax carving sets', rather than branded cannabis-specific dab tools, to save some cash (but still make sure they are stainless steel or titanium).

HERB GRINDER

Herb grinder: Cannabis flowers are generally ground before rolling a joint or loading a bowl, so a whole array of cannabis-specific devices known as herb grinders exist. Resembling a big hockey puck, these grinders are made of metal, wood or plastic and have top and bottom halves, with an interior lined with spikes. The herb is placed inside the grinder and the top and bottom are turned back and forth between your hands until the herb is ground. The grinder is then opened and the contents are tapped out onto a rolling surface. You can use a herb grinder for cooking purposes too, especially for small-scale applications. Go for a metal one, over plastic or wood, as the teeth are far stronger and the (hopefully) super-sticky herb you're loading into it is less likely to gum it up and break the teeth.

SLOW COOKER

Baking parchment: Useful for storing sticky cannabis oils, parchment also has a variety of uses in a cannabis kitchen, from lining baking trays and tins to pressing rosin.

Silicone baking mats: Sticky hash won't cling to silicone, so get a variety of sizes of silicone baking mats, traditionally used for lining baking trays. Now manufactured for the cannabis market

by a variety of companies, these mats help keep surfaces free of difficult-to-clean oil stains but also make it easy to handle some of the more tacky consistencies.

Slow cooker: Handy for simmering infusions for a long time at a low temperature.

Spice ball or tea strainer: A large, spherical spice ball or tea strainer is convenient for cannabis infusions, as you can add the weed to the strainer, immerse it in a big pot of oil or melted butter, and then easily remove it later.

If you're serious about cooking with weed, here's a bunch of transcendent equipment to acquire.

DECARBOXYLATION
MACHINE

Automatic infusion machine: Set-it-and-forget-it infusion machines are the future, with several appliances on the market that remove the guesswork from infusing cannabis flowers or extracts into fats, glycerine or alcohol. Some of the most advanced infusion machines can even strain out the cannabis material afterwards, making the whole process a truly simple, low-mess affair. Two well-known brands are the MagicalButter machine, which has settings for creating infusions and tinctures with different kinds of fat, and the elegant LEVO machine, which infuses cannabis into oil or melted butter and then even strains it for you.

Decarboxylation machine: If you really want to live large, buy a dedicated decarboxylation machine. The Ardent Lift (NOVA) decarboxylator is a brilliant new invention that activates THC precisely.

Grape press: This device is normally used to juice grapes, but you can also use it to juice the last little bit of cannabinoid content out of your infusion material.

PELLET SMOKER

Smoking gun or pellet smoker: You can add smoke to food by using a smoking gun or pellet smoker (though you need a lot of cannabis to make a pellet smoker work); both methods are more about adding flavour than actually getting weed into things. If a little smoky flavour and some tableside flash are all you want, you can pipe smoke under a cloche to dress up oysters on ice.

The Pot Pantry

The *Bong Appétit* pot pantry is huge, wildly expensive and awe-inspiring. A walk-in weed closet tucked into the corner of the show's test kitchen, it houses more than 30 types of high-end cannabis strains, a dizzying array of hash and extracts and tons of other infused and concentrated ingredients like oils, spices, terpenes and distillates – all collected directly from California's finest producers. It's basically the equivalent to having a fully stocked private dispensary on hand at all times, only with a wider selection and more cutting-edge options.

Obviously, you don't need all that to get started cooking with weed. But it doesn't hurt to know what's out there before diving in. Let's start with the most familiar forms of cannabis and then get weirder.

Flower

The form of dried cannabis that's typically ground and rolled into a joint or smoked in a pipe is known as 'flower' since it is literally the flowers of the cannabis plant. The plant itself is unique because it produces both male and female flowers, with the former pollinating the latter. However, only female cannabis flowers produce significant amounts of the high-inducing cannabinoid THC found in the plant's resin, so growers typically separate females from males early in the cultivation process and allow them to mature to their full splendour without ever going to seed.

Depending on the variety and its growing conditions, flower – sometimes called 'bud', 'nugget' or just 'nug' – can vary widely in potency from 10 to 30 per cent THC content, with variation found

TRICHOMES

SUGAR LEAF

FLOWER

TRIM

NODE

FAN LEAF

STALK

even within different parts of the same plant. The biggest bud on top of a plant is called the 'cola', and it receives the most energy from light. That means it grows larger and generally has a higher quantity of the desirable psychoactive resin than do the smaller buds on the lower branches. Typically, the best buds are dried, cured and reserved for smoking, while the smaller, less potent 'popcorn nugs' that appear towards the often-shaded bottom and centre of the plant are relegated to culinary use or extraction. As cannabis costs fall with the increase in legal production, cooks will be able to source and utilise different and higher-quality cannabis ingredients. That includes flowers cultivated using specific methods (e.g., organic, vegan), the sourcing of specific varietals that offer special aromatic or flavour qualities and also the utilisation of high-flavour or high-potency cannabis extracts.

Why are cannabis extracts better culinary ingredients than flower? Well, all green parts of the cannabis plant contain chlorophyll, responsible for the 'grassy' taste most people associate with weed food. Refining flowers into hash or extracts before use in food removes most, if not all, of this chlorophyll and makes for a tastier, more refined final product.

Flower can be used in cooking when it is freshly harvested (especially for juicing), but is generally utilised after it has been dried and cured for smoking. Cannabis flower won't get you high on its own as it needs to be decarboxylated (exposed to heat) for the THCA present in the flower to be converted into THC, its psychoactive form. Once activated, the decarboxylated cannabis needs to be infused into fats, sugars or alcohol, although technically it can be eaten on its own and still have an effect. (On the show, they frequently crisp broken flowers in fat and then use the cooked bud fragments to garnish other dishes.)

Trim

Also known as 'sugar leaf', trim is the industry term for the small leaves, near the buds, that are trimmed away when flowers are manicured for sale after harvest. Traditionally used for making cost-effective edibles, trim contains significant amounts of THC

Comparison of Raw Cannabis Ingredients: Flower, Trim and Kief

Type of Cannabis Ingredient		THC Percentage by Weight	THC Content	Acidic THC Content
Flower: Forbidden Fruit strain (dried and cured)		9.05	3.2mg/g	99.5mg/g
Trim: Forbidden Fruit strain (dried and cured)		3.68	2.4mg/g	39.2mg/g
Kief: Forbidden Fruit strain		55	44.6mg/g	584mg/g

and other cannabinoids that would otherwise be wasted. Considered too harsh for smoking and too fibrous just to eat, these leaves can be used to make hash or infused directly into fats for cooking. High-quality trim can test up to 15 per cent THC, with lower-quality samples measuring between 2 and 5 per cent THC, making it a much lower-potency product than flower.

Like flower, trim can be used fresh and raw or after being dried and cured. Also like flower, trim must be decarboxylated before its THC content is fully available. Trim delivers more chlorophyll because the plant matter has been snipped apart, often creating a grassier taste when infused, compared to flower.

Fan Leaves

The large, iconic cannabis leaves gather solar energy for plant growth, which means they contain copious amounts of chlorophyll and only trace amounts of THCA. Fan leaves are also fibrous and tough, so they can be hard to digest when fully grown. If you're looking to eat them raw in a pesto or salad, choose young, tender leaves from a plant in an early stage of growth; their flavour lands somewhere between kale and shiso, with slight variations in flavour based on the strain. Unfortunately, you can't buy a bag of baby pot leaves at Whole Foods yet, so you'll need to grow them yourself or source them directly from the farmer.

Although they're not recommended for edibles, fan leaves can be used for the cannabis leaf crisps on page 220, the kimchi on page 234, and the candied leaves in 'Vanessa Says' on page 213. Fan leaves can also be juiced for a rich source of acidic cannabinoids that won't get you high. The acidic precursor to THC is known as THCA, and it provides a variety of medicinal benefits, such as anti-inflammatory and anti-emetic properties, without psychoactive effects. The juice can be mixed into cocktails or frozen into ice pops. The most common use for fan leaves, however, is as a garnish or as part of a table decoration, as they really help your dinner party say, 'This food has weed in it.'

Leaves are highly perishable. Like any other fresh herb or cut flower, they begin to wither and dry out quickly if not kept in a properly humid environment. Wrap their stems in a damp paper towel, seal in a plastic bag and then refrigerate to maintain freshness. You can also store the leaves or small shoots with stems in a glass of water in the fridge for a few days, like you do with coriander or basil. Fan leaves are almost always used raw, and their THC content is so low as not to be worth trying to decarb for infusing.

Trichomes

While you won't see a container labelled 'trichomes' in the *Bong Appétit* pantry, these tiny resin glands are scattered throughout the cannabis plant – particularly on its buds – where the majority of the plant's THC can be found. To the naked eye, these glands look like glittery crystals and they are responsible for the frosty appearance of top-shelf flower. When magnified, they look like sphere-topped stalks – crystal mushrooms from another planet. These resin-filled spheres are the most desirable part of the cannabis plant and are responsible for the vast majority of its effects, as well as its aroma and flavour, thanks to the rich essential oils packed into the heads. They are harvested and concentrated into hash and various types of extracts using a variety of techniques that involve solvents, such as CO_2 or butane or iced water.

Considered a raw cannabis ingredient, trichomes that have been separated from the plant matter and collected en masse are referred to as 'kief' (see below), which must be decarboxylated in order to develop its psychoactive THC content fully. The two traditional forms of hash, compressed bricks and balls, are made entirely of kief.

Kief

A sand-like, light brown powder, kief is one of the most traditional methods of concentrating cannabis, with origins stretching back thousands of years to the vast cannabis fields of India, Morocco and Pakistan. Kief is simply a collection of trichomes that have been separated from the cannabis plant by 'dry sifting' – shaking buds or trim so that the trichome glands fall through fine fabric or metal screens. You can collect kief at home, but it's easier to buy it, as accumulating enough kief to use for cooking would take quite a long time. Every time you grind a flower, kief is separated from the plant matter and either sticks to the inside of the grinder or appears as a fine powder on your rolling tray. Many herb grinder models include a 'kief catcher', a chamber separated from the grinding compartment by an ultrafine screen.

With each grind, a small amount of kief is deposited into this chamber for later use.

Kief is one of the most versatile ways to use cannabis as an ingredient, as it can be stirred into or sprinkled onto dishes just like most spices. But at fifteen dollars (£11) per gram in the US, it is currently more expensive than saffron. Once cannabis is cultivated on a much larger scale, prices will likely fall and terpene-rich kief, which can carry the unique, vibrant flavours of various cannabis strains into every dish, will become much more widely available.

Although kief is considered a raw cannabis ingredient, it may have low amounts of psychoactive THC because it has often been dried and cured or otherwise handled enough to cause partial THCA conversion. To activate the THC in these dry-sifted trichomes fully, decarboxylation, or 'toasting' the kief (see page 54), is required.

1 – **AGITATE CANNABIS
FLOWER WITH ICED WATER**

2 – **DRAIN THROUGH A SERIES
OF ICE-O-LATOR BAGS**

3 – **SPREAD OVER A BAKING
TRAY AND LET DRY**

4 – **JAR AND CURE
BEFORE SERVING**

Water Hash

Hash is a catch-all term for concentrated and isolated trichomes prepared in a traditional fashion, either by dry sifting and then using a combination of heat and pressure, or by a water-based extraction method. Hash can appear as a granulated powder that looks like brown sugar, as pressed chunks of trichomes stuck together, or as a smooth, polished, potent temple ball, the age-old Nepalese form still created today by artisans such as Frenchy Cannoli.

While hash can be made using a variety of methods, the most common modern technique for physically separating trichomes from plant matter is known as water, or ice, hash. When cannabis flowers and/or trim are agitated together with iced water, the trichomes grow brittle and break off from the plant matter. Though water hash is commonly made using dried plant material, artisans have also started using fresh-frozen plants, which many believe provide a much stronger aroma and flavour due to the higher concentrations of terpenes. Next, the loose trichomes are separated from the water by passing the water through a set of increasingly fine-mesh microscreen bags. The resulting mass is collected, dried and cured, at which point it is ready for smoking or cooking. Some hash makers grate these chunks on a microplane grater to increase surface area, speed up drying and prevent mould from forming in the interior. Water hash is known by several different names, including 'ice wax', 'bubble hash' and 'full melt'.

Hash usually needs to be decarboxylated before cooking to fully activate all of its THC content. In its raw form, it does often contain a small percentage of THC, however, created during the

drying and curing process. You can use water hash in any recipe that calls for kief, but you'll need to grate it or crumble it into a fine powder to ensure even distribution. A microplane grater is the best tool for working with hard chunks of hash, while other types crumble easily when chopped with a knife.

The best hash has amazing varietal-specific flavour that can greatly enhance dishes. Medium- and lower-grade hash is still a more pure and concentrated form of cannabis compared to flower, and generally provides a cleaner, less obtrusive flavour free of the harsh, bitter, chlorophyll taste that can come from flower.

Concentrates and Extracts

Highly concentrated cannabis extracts are made by using either hydrocarbon solvents or CO_2 to strip all the stuff that doesn't get you high from the stuff that does. What remains is a resinous extract of ultrapure cannabinoids, terpenoids and flavonoids, which come in a bunch of different textures based on the post-extraction processes.

These extracts are primarily consumed via 'dabbing', which means scooping up a small amount and dropping it on a heated surface attached to a water pipe known as a 'dab rig'. Extracts can also be consumed in vaporisers, with the portable cartridge pen-style units being the most popular.

Cooking with extracts is a rare treat; it allows you to dose your food and control cannabis flavours incredibly precisely. Extracts are

High-end water hashes from Rezn Extracts display a variety of colours and textures. Clockwise from top: Fine-grade Elmer's Glue, Cookies rosin, Candyland, a coarser grade of Elmer's Glue, Sour Grapes, Kosher Kush rosin and Cookies.

expensive – sometimes ranging from £45 (US$60) to more than £75 (US$100) per gram – and precious, so you probably won't be cooking with them all that often.

The following are the most common types of extracts on the market.

- **BHO**, short for butane hash oil, is made by using butane as a solvent to dissolve cannabinoids away from plant matter. Propane or other mixed-gas blends can also be used in the same way. This method of extraction is used in many industries, including for aloe, aspirin and perfumes. BHO extracts generally contain between 65 and 80 per cent THCA content.

- **Budder** or **Wax** has an opaque texture created through a post-extraction whipping process that creates an emulsion along with other aroma and flavour compounds such as terpenes. The texture gives the product its name; a softer, smoother, stickier consistency is generally referred to as 'budder', while a drier, more crumbly consistency is known as 'wax' or 'crumble'.

- **Distillates** are tasteless, odourless, up to 99 per cent pure, and are often used for edible products in which no cannabis taste is desired. Distillate is extracted through a basic chemical evaporation process similar to the way alcohol is refined, with each step removing more impurities and undesired compounds. THC and CBDA distillate are the most common distillates found on the market.

- **Isolate** is any single molecule extraction, usually THCA or CBD. It generally comes in a crystalline form and is grown in a scientific glass vessel; just like those crystal kits you had as a kid. While incredibly useful for precise dosing of edibles, isolate is devoid of any other cannabinoids or terpenes, leading to a highly singular effect that many argue lacks the character (and sometimes medicinal qualities) of a multimolecule product.

- **Live resin** is a terpene-rich extract from freshly harvested plants that are quickly frozen, ideally using a cryogenic freezer. By capturing the plant at its aromatic peak, the extractor is able to create a concentrate with higher percentages of terpenes than a product made from dried plant material. Live resin is made using butane or propane, though there is also 'live rosin' or 'frosin', which is rosin made using fresh-frozen kief that has been sifted away from the plants. Live resin can take many forms, including budder, crystalline, sauce, shatter and sugar, depending on how it is handled post-extraction. Live resin tends to have less THCA than concentrates made from dry material because it has more terpenes in the mix, so it generally tests between 60 and 75 per cent THCA.

- **Rosin** is created from either flowers or hash, which are extruded into a concentrate using just pressure and heat. At-home hash-makers tend to utilise hair straighteners for small-batch production, though many companies have begun selling large-scale extractor units capable of tons of pressure and with customisable heat settings, allowing extractors to find the perfect press. Rosin can be made from dry or fresh-frozen material, though the latter is usually created from kief or water hash because fresh buds cannot be pressed cleanly. While it has seemingly just come into vogue in the last couple of years, rosin is actually based on an ancient African extraction process involving conical baskets and heat from the sun. The texture of rosin can be clear like shatter but tends to become opaque quickly and ends up with a budder, wax or sugary consistency. Like most extracts, it can take on almost any texture with varying amounts of heat and pressure. Rosin is usually between 55 and 75 per cent THCA, though some extractors have figured out a way to separate out 99+ per cent pure THCA using rosin-based processes.

- **Sauce** is a newer texture that has stolen the spotlight, thanks in large part to its gorgeous appearance. It's a mix of THCA crystals of varying size (often called 'diamonds' when they reach a certain size and distinctness) floating in a 'sauce' of extremely aromatic terpenes and flavonoids between 30 and 50 per cent THCA. This sauce portion is often referred to as HTFSE, or high terpene full spectrum extract, while the crystal portion is often called HTFCE, or high terpene full cannabinoid extract.

- **Shatter** is a clear concentrate generally made using BHO processes, though rosin sometimes takes on this consistency as well. Shatter can be very brittle and break apart like glass (hence the name) or it can be more sticky like sap, depending on the terpenes present in the extract and also the ambient temperature. To make sappy shatter brittle and easier to handle, you can cool it by placing it between two cold surfaces. Shatter is usually between 60 and 80 per cent THCA, depending on quality.

Dabbing concentrate onto a hot surface or smoking flower by burning it instantly decarboxylates it before the resulting smoke is inhaled. Cannabis extracts and flower must both be decarboxylated for cooking in order to activate THC fully, and you can do this by toasting them in the oven (see page 54), heating in a saucepan, or with the 'sous vide' method (see page 58) or jar method (used in chapter 1, see page 65). The only exception to this rule is THC distillate, which is already activated and can simply be added to recipes or consumed directly.

Terpenes

Naturally occurring chemical components found in cannabis and many other plants, terpenes are what make weed smell (and taste) the way it does. They can be anything from citrusy, skunky, piney or just straight-up dank. Terpenes from cannabis strains can be isolated and bottled, capturing the plant's essence for adding to drinks or dishes to imbue them with a distinct cannabis flavour but no high.

Used in cooking just like essential oils derived from plants such as mint or basil, these compounds deliver sensorial delights without any of the usual psychoactive effects of cannabis. It's worth mentioning with terpenes that a little goes a long way – one drop of terpenes can, at times, be enough to flavour an entire dish, depending on the strain's flavour profile and pungence. Terpenes can be purchased online, but cannabis-derived terpenes are expensive and not so easy to come by. You can easily find terpenes derived from other sources (such as pine trees or lemons), but these are not necessarily recommended for smoking or even adding to

food because they are primarily created for aromatic applications such as aromatherapy atomisers. Make sure to read the labels for any terpenes to determine the types of use for which the specific product was created.

Terpenes (which are explored in-depth starting on page 43) provide the 'flavour profile' of a cannabis strain, allowing for both the art and science of pairing weed strains (like wines) with food and for incorporating a specific strain into a recipe (like the Double-Lemon Roast Chicken on page 165 made with Lemon Skunk strain).

How to Go Weed Shopping

Wandering into an LA dispensary can be a little intimidating, even for the practised pothead. Jars full of fuzzy, sparkling flowers in various shades of green; small containers of translucent amber extracts; and prepackaged edibles of every possible variety crowd the shelves, making it tough to determine exactly what you need – especially if you're new to cooking with cannabis. Based on your budget, you'll be looking to buy kief, hash, extracts, infused oils or butters, flowers or trim for cannabis cooking projects. So whether it's the first time you've been to the pot store or it's your 420th visit, here's how to pick the perfect pot.

Bud Basics: Sativa vs. Indica

The distinctions between the two basic subspecies of cannabis – sativa and indica – have perhaps been overstated, especially since most of what's on the market is actually a hybrid of the two. It's basically a cliché that sativa strains are stimulating and cerebral, better for creative work or gaming, while an indica delivers a more relaxing or sedating body high.

Over the years, growers have crossed the two types extensively, looking for best-of-both-worlds progeny. Such hybrid strains have come to dominate the market so thoroughly that when a varietal is described as either sativa or indica, it's most likely an indicator of which genetics are dominant in the cross.

That said, some people respond much differently to sativa-dominant strains than to indica-dominant strains. And if that's

These award-winning cannabis flowers from Purple Frost Genetics in Santa Cruz, California have subtle differences from bud to bud.

you, definitely source the one that matches the mood you'd like to set. Heading out for a hike through the wilderness? Sativa. Wanting to unwind after a long day at work? Indica. Try to source varieties as close to 100 per cent of one or the other to emphasise the desired effect.

At the time of writing, there is no legal or regulatory mechanism that requires producers to prove if a strain is sativa or indica; the genetics of most marijuana strains are murky at best. That means your best bet is to chat with the employees at your dispensary to figure out what is what.

How to Know What You'll Like

How do you know which weed is the one for you? You'll smell it! The type of cannabis that smells best to you is almost always the one with a high that you'll enjoy.

Increasingly, research points to the presence and combination of different terpenes as significantly influencing the effects of various strains. That means the future of cannabis classification is going to be much more complex and multifaceted than our current sativa/indica dichotomy. The distinction between the two is more relevant to cultivators and breeders, while consumers should begin to focus on the varying terpene profiles and 'strain fingerprints' that truly determine how the variety makes them feel a certain kind of stoned.

For instance, it seems like strains with a significant amount of limonene (see page 50) tend to confer a high that's uplifting and creative – an effect traditionally attributed to the sativa subspecies.

How Legitimate Are Strain Names?

Literally tens of thousands of named cannabis strains exist, and 90 per cent of the excitement around specific strains is little more than marketing hype. Sorry to burst anyone's bubble, but dispensary staff will randomly change the name of a strain to something that sounds better if the stuff isn't moving out the door.

Say you have a friend in Santa Cruz who grows weed, and she gives you an amazing jar of Black Cherry Pie that smoked awesomely, smelled terrific, and gave you a great high. Seeking to replicate the experience while travelling, you go somewhere else and buy some Black Cherry Pie, only to be disappointed when it doesn't give you the same type of high.

That scenario happens all of the time, and it's because the experience of a specific strain isn't just about the genetics. It's also about the *terroir* (the land and environmental factors affecting a crop) and the skill of the cultivator. The Black Cherry Pie you liked so much should really be called 'Sarah's Santa Cruz Black Cherry Pie, Plant #207, Harvested on October 27', and it might have resonated with you because the terpene profile was expertly preserved during the curing process, an organic fertiliser regimen allowed the plant to express its best flavours fully, and the production of resin glands (trichomes) was maximised under the bright California sun during an exceptional Santa Cruz season. Much like wine, cannabis will smell, taste and produce different effects depending upon how it is grown and handled throughout its life cycle. A grower can cultivate 'the perfect plant' only to have it stored and cured improperly by someone down the line, which can totally destroy the flavour and smoking experience. Each step of the process is as important as the one that came before it.

Cannabis strains are created by growers and breeders, much like tomato or rose varieties in traditional horticulture. When done properly, seed breeding involves selecting for the hardiest plants most capable of thriving in a specific environment, or for plants that have a unique flavour profile, and the process of honing in on the best specimens is refined over many years. To have the most value as a consistent identifier, you must source strains directly from the breeder. Get your genetics from a reputable seed bank and you're much more likely to find the consistent cannabis you're looking for.

With this understanding, when you're seeking to replicate a previously enjoyed high, either source from the same producer or seek out the same genetics grown in the same region in the original style. Or just trust your nose and smoke or eat the weed that smells the best to you.

Clone-Only vs. Seed Varieties

Another key piece of understanding why a certain cannabis strain makes you feel a certain way is knowing the difference between clone-only and from-seed plants. For example, the strain Golden Goat is a specific individual plant, chosen by the breeder from a handful of seeds and preserved via cloning, or asexual propagation, since the late 2000s. In exactly the same way cuttings are taken from tomato

plants, growers take cuttings from cannabis 'mother plants' in order to create exact genetic replicas of their favourite varieties. This allows for repeatable results across a large number of plants, making it easier to dial in the way strains are grown, as well as produce a lot of one specific product. Most strains on US dispensary shelves are actually just individual plants chosen by their grower and kept over time.

In contrast, varieties such as Super Lemon Haze, White Widow and Deadhead OG have been released by seed companies. This means there are now literally thousands of different plants called 'Super Lemon Haze' that resulted from the same parents, but all of which still have the potential to express different traits. While good breeders are able to produce seeds that provide a fairly repeatable experience, genetically there is still a huge variety of possibilities contained within each individual seed, making it difficult for a customer to know what they are getting every time. If you're not familiar with a strain, ask for its lineage and whether it is clone-only or from seed; you will then have a better idea of how repeatable your experience will be with that particular variety.

How to Know If the Weed Is Good

If you are unable to officially hammer down the strain that you're smoking, the least you can do is make sure that whatever it is, it's good quality. Always ask if you can open jars and sniff the merchandise because scent is usually the best indication of quality cannabis. Pass on any offering that smells musty or of harsh chemicals. These indicators can mean that a strain wasn't flushed properly before harvest, or that it was rushed to market and may have become mouldy along the way because it wasn't properly dried and cured.

But if your test meets with a strong, pleasant aroma, then it's reasonable to assume the pot was grown and processed correctly. What you're smelling are the terpenes – THC doesn't have much of a smell on its own – and they are the best way to determine quality flowers.

Next, use a magnifying glass or microscope – which a dispensary or real overachiever of a dealer should have handy – to look at the quality and preservation of the trichomes and confirm the absence of mould, which looks like fuzzy white or grey patches. Using your naked eye, look at the bud for signs of discoloration as well as gouges from overzealous trimmers. While the presence of some leaf is okay, modern cannabis is trimmed thoroughly for a reason; the presence of leaf matter makes for a harsher smoke, so look for well-trimmed buds that are free of 'crow's feet' leaves curling around the sides. Finally, the buds should ideally be sticky and firm to the touch, yielding to a slight squeeze. They should not be so dry that they break apart under slight pressure, although you can still consume bud in that condition. Storing cannabis properly in dry environments is especially important, as a place with low relative humidity can turn a properly squishy bud into a dust pile waiting to happen in a matter of hours.

The dispensary staff are usually not going to let you touch or handle buds, so you can ask the budtender to squeeze it with their gloved hands for you.

Looking for trim? All the same tips apply as far as inspecting for mould and trusting your nose. Some dispensaries sell trim, and others don't, so call ahead to make sure. The best source for trim is from a friendly grower or your own plants. While it generally is less pungent-smelling than buds, trim should still have a distinct aroma and should never smell like hay or vegetation. Look for the presence of visible trichomes, and always ask if the trim is 'hand trim' as opposed to 'machine trim', as a hand-trimmed product is handled more carefully and usually has a far higher cannabinoid content.

When sourcing kief, ask if you can smell it and inspect for mould. Kief should be a light sandy colour; a green tint indicates a sub-par extraction process that introduced too much plant matter. When evaluating other concentrates, ask the staff who crafted the concentrate, as well as what solvent was used. Concentrates (other than whole-plant ethanol-extracted oil intended for oral ingestion, often called RSO, or Rick Simpson Oil) should never be black or green. Extracts are generally of acceptable quality when they are white, golden, orange or amber, and they should also smell distinctly like the strain(s) from which they were extracted. Many dispensaries will be able to provide you with lab test results for their products that show the cannabinoid content (THCA, THC, CBD, CBN usually) as well as residual solvents for concentrates (expressed in parts per million), and even the individual terpenes present in the sample. Lab testing is not perfect and should not be the sole determining factor for quality but, along with these other tools, can help to inform your cannabis buying decisions.

WHAT TO ASK AT THE DISPENSARY

When you visit your dispensary, ask the following questions to ensure that you leave with exactly the product you want.

— What's fresh today?

You want a recent batch of cannabis, not something that's been sitting on the shelf for too long.

— Is there anything that smells like oranges or lemons?

If you usually like citrusy cannabis, start there. If you tend towards floral or sweet-smelling strains, ask for strains that give off those aromas.

— What's good for an active day? What's good for sleep?

Asking if a strain supports specific effects will help you find the product you most enjoy.

— What do you have for my budget?

Being specific about your price point can greatly speed up a consultation. Dispensary staff don't want to offer you options that you can't afford.

— Is this sun grown or indoor? Was it fed with traditional nutrients or was it grown organically?

If you're looking for eco-friendly cannabis, make sure it was grown outdoors or in a greenhouse, which runs on much less energy than a warehouse full of high-intensity discharge lamps. Plus, cannabis nurtured in a living soil and fed compost can be much more flavourful. As you consume cannabis grown using different nutrients and in diverse growing mediums (soil, coco coir, mineral wool, pure hydroponic, aeroponic, etc.), you'll become more familiar with what you like and don't.

— Is this lab tested? Can I see a terpene profile?

Most dispensaries must test their cannabis for THC potency and to confirm products are free of pesticide residue. Some places also test for terpene profiles, but not all. So, for example, so if you're looking for a strain high in limonene, you might have to rely on your nose.

Get It Farm Fresh

There's an expanding organic-pot movement afoot, with master cannabis growers tailoring their cultivation methods to specific weed strains to coax the best aromas and flavours out of their bud. Just like farmers' market produce, pot from a good grower makes a world of difference.

Complicating the issue is the fact that the United States Department of Agriculture (USDA) determines what can be called 'organic' via on-site inspection, and since cannabis is still illegal in the eyes of the federal government, it cannot be legally inspected, labelled or sold as USDA organic.

Third-party certification services in the US, including Clean Green, Certified Kind and the Cannabis Certification Council, have sprung up to identify eco-friendly cannabis growers and distinguish their products from competitors, so be sure to ask your dispensary if it carries any cannabis that has been verified as environmentally sound.

Indoor vs. Outdoor

It's a common misconception that cannabis grown indoors is automatically superior to cannabis grown outdoors; songs about 'indo' or 'hydro' notwithstanding. The skill of the farmer and the quality of the plant's genetics is the main determining factor in whether or not cannabis is good, not just where it was grown.

The most photogenic and aromatic buds tend to come from indoor farms powered by high-intensity artificial lights (much like those hothouse tomatoes grown in Holland), which means they typically fetch premium prices at market. But there's also an increasing movement to support small, eco-friendly cannabis farmers raising 'sun grown', or outdoor, weed. Many connoisseurs believe that the sun's rays cause the plants to produce different compounds and greatly increase their vigour, leading to a product that can have a higher medicinal and flavour potential when cultivated properly.

Much like the farm-to-table movement in food, going small and organic when buying weed allows you to incorporate top-quality herb into your cooking while supporting artisanal growers following best practices. With more brands available than ever before, do a little research into who grew your weed and where. The best weed is grown in small batches by people who care about it and who have honed their methods over years of experience. Much like craft brews, bean-to-bar chocolate and fine wine, there are no shortcuts when it comes to growing, harvesting, drying and curing primo weed.

Weed Storage

Once you get your cannabis home from the dispensary, you need to keep it as fresh as possible. Cannabis flowers, hash and extracts all benefit from being stored in a cool, dry, dark place. Some connoisseurs store their extracts in a wine fridge, which helps preserve flavours and aromas that evaporate over time or when exposed to light and heat.

Choose an airtight, opaque glass jar for long-term storage of cannabis flowers and try to use your flowers within three months. Old cannabis will turn golden yellow, and its aroma loses nuance, becoming much like hay or old grass clippings.

Extracts also begin to degrade as they age depending on how they are stored, and many types of concentrate become more volatile. Both temperature and humidity can cause changes in consistency over time. High terpene extracts such as live resin and fresh-frozen rosin are highly perishable because terpenes evaporate easily, so it's usually best to enjoy these products as quickly as possible.

The exception to the short-term storage rule is artisanally produced hashes and temple balls made in the traditional fashion, which can benefit from a long cure that develops flavour. Kief and most types of water hash should ideally be used within three months.

In the Cannabis Lab

In making and testing infusions for this book, we consulted with Dr Jeff Raber from The Werc Shop, a prestigious cannabis lab in Southern California. The lab tests products using an analytical chemistry method known as high-performance liquid chromatography (HPLC), which can separate, identify and quantify each component in a mixture. Without the benefit of the equipment that makes this technique possible, professional edibles manufacturers would be unable to determine THC content precisely.

So how can home cooks get the most bang for their buck out of weed? Dr Raber says it helps to be methodical and pay attention to details every step of the way. 'Standardisation at home is exceptionally challenging,' he explains. 'There are a lot of variables on which you have no insight and no way to double-check.'

For starters, are you working with any reliable test values whatsoever? Even if your cannabis is sold as having 25 per cent THC, in reality that value might be much lower. 'Is that test value representative of the 5 grams that you bought? Maybe; maybe not,' Raber says.

Why is this? Well, the inherent nature of plant material is not homogeneous. Cannabis flowers have many little nooks and crannies where THC can hide, and there's variation in potency from the top of the plant, which gets a lot of light to maximise resin production, and the bottom of the plant, where flowers are less potent. All of this means that different parts of the same cannabis plant can vary from 15 to 25 per cent THC.

Sparkling trichomes containing THC and other cannabinoids cover this batch of Platinum Girl Scout Cookies grown by Kyle Kushman.

Concentrates are much more homogeneous due to the absence of plant matter, making them better suited to cooking consistent batches of edibles and estimating potency at home. Concentrates are also nice because you can use very small amounts thanks to their high potency levels, making it easier to hide the cannabis flavour if so desired. Also, despite their higher per-gram price, concentrates are generally almost the same value proposition as using flowers for cooking because you can use so little at a time.

As far as infusion methods go, Raber says that 'the mason-jar method is pretty efficient as far as we've seen. It depends on the heat and how long you do it, but I haven't been able to do a lot of tests on the spent plant material.' Doing what's known as a 'mass balance test' to measure the THC left behind is the only way to know if all of the cannabinoids were captured and how efficient the infusion was.

Cannabinoids

When we get lab test results, what we're looking for are the levels of different cannabinoids found in flowers, trim, kief, hash and other ingredients used in a cannabis kitchen. The cannabis plant owes both its medicinal benefits and its pleasant high to a set of compounds called cannabinoids that are virtually unique to the species. Blending THC and CBD to desired effect is already established practice among cannabis-adept chefs, and every day our understanding of weed's remaining eighty-plus cannabinoids grows through experimentation.

Some cannabinoids, like THC, THCA and CBD, can be found in isolated, purified forms, including crystalline and distillate extracts. When reading test results, other cannabinoids will be listed, and it's helpful to know their effects and properties when you're evaluating specific products. High amounts of CBDA and THCV are found in certain cannabis strains, with varying ratios present in all cannabis products derived from whole plants. The following are the most commonly known and studied cannabinoids, which can help boost your understanding of the scientific complexities of whole-plant medicine.

CBD Lesser known but gaining quickly in popularity, CBD is shorthand for cannabidiol. A non-euphoric component of cannabis, CBD has anti-inflammatory benefits and aids in muscle relaxation and lowering anxiety. CBD also tempers the anxiety that can sometimes result from THC, preventing it from becoming too overwhelming. High levels of CBD can be found in certain strains, such as Harlequin, ACDC and Sour Tsunami, and its presence would also be in the extracts or infusions made from these strains.

CBDA The acidic form of CBD is present in freshly harvested high-CBD cannabis strains and can be made available through juicing or extraction. Like THCA and its activated form, THC, CBDA is converted to CBD via decarboxylation (heat and time) when infused or smoked.

CBG Cannabigerol (CBG) is a minor cannabinoid, but it seems to have a big impact on fighting tumor growth. It's also particularly effective at killing bacteria and reducing inflammation.

CBN Cannabinol (CBN) is a degraded form of THC and THCA that results from oxidation or UV light exposure. Heating your infusions for too long or at too high a temperature will cause the THC to convert into CBN, which is a known sedative. So if you're looking for a natural sleep aid, CBN is wonderful. Otherwise, it's usually a sign that you need to fine-tune your infusion process.

THC Short for Delta-9-tetrahydrocannabinol, this magic molecule is what started the love affair between humanity and weed. Responsible for the euphoria, giggles and good times we all associate with being high, THC is the main psychoactive component in cannabis flowers, trim, kief, hash and all types of products made with these ingredients.

THCA This is the inactive, acidic form of THC found in living plants, as well as cured buds and trim. While some hash and concentrates have small amounts of THC present, they are also primarily THCA, which becomes THC when smoked or decarboxylated for infusion. THCA possesses many of the same healing qualities as THC, but because it has not yet been 'decarb'ed' (that is, decarboxylated), it is not psychoactive. Look for THCA in certain tinctures or capsule products formulated to possess healing effects without the psychedelic high of activated THC.

THCV A rarely occurring cannabinoid with an interesting effect, tetrahydrocannabivarin (THCV) may have appetite suppression properties, leading to conjecture that a strain of 'skinny weed' could be created to actively encourage weight loss. Only a small percentage of strains have any THCV presence, but there may be many more that are just waiting to be discovered.

Dosing

First off, it's basically impossible to eat so much THC that you die. In the US, Colorado's recommended dose (which most other legal states have followed) for edibles is 10 milligrams of active THC per serving. It's estimated that a 80-kg (175-pound) man would need to eat 53 grams of pure THC in one sitting to reach a fatal dose. That's an occurrence so unheard-of as to be theoretical; as long as you aren't shooting tons of pure THC right into your bloodstream, you'll survive.

Although THC is much safer than alcohol, caffeine and nicotine, it can definitely make your heart race, inducing anxiety and panic attacks if you eat too much, so go slowly and learn your limits. If you accidentally go overboard, it could take a while – and maybe a few freak-outs – before the fog begins to lift.

In states where pot is legal, store-bought edibles are routinely lab tested for potency and are accurately labelled with suggested serving sizes. Knowing the cannabinoid content has been a huge game changer for all of the people who swore off edibles forever after a bad experience. Even if you don't have access to a fancy weed lab, there are a few steps you can take to make sure your at-home dosing is manageable.

When making your own infusions, follow the instructions in this book carefully and be sure to double-check your maths. And always round up when estimating THC content, assuming there is more pot in a recipe than you might think. Why? The difference between a very pleasant edibles experience and a very unpleasant one can hinge on consuming just 10 milligrams more THC than planned for, so why not err on the side of caution? You can always eat more; you can never eat less.

Vanessa Says: If you've never cooked with cannabis before, just keep in mind that a little can go a long way. It's easy to throw a bunch of flowers into butter and make a potent edible. Patience and restraint only means you get to eat more edibles until you find the right dose for you. My first time in the kitchen, I chose the other path. It was a 420 I'll never remember.

If you're in a legal state, you can skip a couple of steps here and just buy pre-made infusions. Weed-infused butters, oils, honeys and chocolates are all widely available at finer pot shops and can easily be incorporated into a wide variety of recipes. Basically, it all comes down to how high you want to get. If you're looking for a gentle 10-milligram dose of THC, find a cannabis chocolate bar with segments dosed appropriately and then melt a piece into your hot cocoa. The same is true for honey: if 1 tablespoon delivers 10 milligrams, drizzle that amount into your tea.

From Microdosing to Greening Out

Finding your minimum effective dose is important, whether you're an experienced edibles consumer or a new user. Discovering the smallest possible amount of THC that causes you to feel effects is possible through trial and error, and knowing your dose will help you avoid having an unpleasant experience. Everyone's body chemistry varies greatly when it comes to the effects of cannabis consumption, and the right dose for you could range anywhere between 5 and 500 milligrams.

Your metabolism, fitness level, diet and other factors come into play in how your body processes and tolerates edibles. For example, athletic people notice effects from smaller amounts of THC because their bodies operate at maximum efficiency. Cannabis works its way through your digestive system before ending up in the liver, where THC is converted into 11-hydroxy-THC, an even more potent chemical.

This in-body chemical conversion doesn't take place when you smoke weed, and it is the reason why edibles are so much more potent and long-lasting than smoking. (When you smoke, the THC is instantly combusted, inhaled through your lungs, and then enters your bloodstream, bypassing your liver.)

A new user of cannabis should begin with no more than 10 milligrams of THC and then wait two hours before taking any more. If you barely feel 10 milligrams, that's fine. Either after two hours or the next time, you can work your way up to 15 or 20 milligrams. Just increase your dose slowly until you find your minimum effective dose.

If you usually buy edibles, you've probably noticed more and more products are intended for microdoses, starting between 2.5 and 5 milligrams of THC, which makes it easier to calibrate the right dose for you. And while you'll see some really potent products containing up to 1,000 milligrams of THC on some dispensary shelves, they're not single-serving doses. They're just cost-effective for people who can pace themselves (and if you're not one of them, you're best off steering clear).

We've designed the recipes in this book to yield individual portions that are satisfying without exceeding your dosage limit. Most of the yields have been adjusted to deliver 5 to 10 milligrams of THC, with explanations on how you can add more if desired. A few of the desserts are dosed slightly higher. That's because if you're going to be indulgent, it might as well be with sweets.

HOW TO EAT WEED FOOD: A BEGINNER'S PRIMER

1. **Start low.** We cannot emphasise this strongly enough. Start at 5 to 10 milligrams and go up slowly until you find your minimum effective dose.

2. **Go slowly.** The classic rookie mistake is eating a dose, eating another a half hour later because you don't feel anything, and then getting too high. Wait at least two hours before going back for seconds.

3. **No booze for beginners.** Yes, we have a cocktails chapter, but that's some expert-level stuff. Eating cannabis and being drunk at the same time is usually awful, unless you happen to love the spins. If you're going to do both, keep it low-key. Eat a tiny bit of THC and stick to just one glass of wine or beer until you know how the combination will make you feel.

4. **Balance THC with CBD.** CBD (see page 34) takes the edge off a THC high, while providing its own sedative and anti-anxiety effects. So ingesting an edible with a 1:1 ratio of THC to CBD will provide a much more chill experience than will THC alone.

5. **Eat real food too.** Eating a light snack immediately before or after an edible will help slow the onset of the effects of THC, as it will take longer to digest and absorb into your body. Conversely, eating weed on an empty stomach will intensify its effects.

6. **Label your THC treats.** Pot food is great. Accidentally eating pot food is the worst. Also, make sure your stash is kept safely away from children and pets.

What to Do If You Eat Too Much THC

Cannabis is a mild psychedelic, and if you've never tripped before, it can be unnerving. If you find yourself too damn high, here are a few proven strategies and anecdotal antidotes for making things right.

Black Peppercorns Chewing on one or two peppercorns (or even just inhaling the scent of freshly ground black pepper) can help assuage the paranoia brought on by too much THC. Beta-caryophyllene, a terpene found in pepper, actually binds to the cannabinoid receptors in your brain and produces a calming effect.

CBD Non-psychoactive CBD (see page 34) acts to temper the high of THC by working on the same cannabinoid receptors in the brain and throughout the body. High-CBD vapes, tinctures and edibles are available and will help you turn the corner if a high grows unmanageable.

Chill Don't stress. Nothing physically dangerous is happening. Find a quiet, dimly lit space and chill. Set an alarm if you need to wake up anytime in the next sixteen hours. Know that even if you get too baked, you will be able to sleep it off and wake up feeling a little groggy but okay.

Eat Food Eating something fatty, like a burger or fries, will help slow down the digestion of THC in your system and dilute the effects somewhat.

Stay Hydrated Drinking plenty of water helps flush the system, and fruit juice or a sugary beverage will raise your blood sugar so you feel more normal.

Vanessa Says: My advice is to make yourself comfortable, have all of your favourite munchies around, put on a funny movie and relax. It'll pass. Of course, if you have a medical condition and are concerned, go to a doctor. But as far as I know, nobody has died from cannabis.

Things to Know About Dosing Cannabis Edibles at Home

For a great many science-based reasons, precisely dosing weed food cooked at home is incredibly difficult. Throughout this book, you'll see the potency of dishes estimated according to the lab results of our infused fats and other active ingredients. That means to replicate the dose level of a recipe at home, you'll need starting material of the same THC potency we used and to follow our directions for decarboxylation and infusion exactly.

Accounting for potential variables like THC potency is also why we made these recipes relatively low dose, so even if the THC dose has a 15 per cent variation, it's still made for lightweights.

Why is it so hard to calculate THC doses in homemade edibles? Efficiency of decarboxylation and infusion methods are two reasons, and then you have to factor in that most foods aren't homogeneous (especially if they are served 'family style') and one part might end up more potent than another. Remember, raw cannabis contains THCA, the acidic version that must be heated to convert into psychoactive THC, so if you can't ensure all the THCA is converted to THC through the decarboxylation and infusion processes, that makes estimating dosage tricky. Theoretically, you should be able to say, 'Well, my

cannabis tested at X per cent THC, so if I put Y grams into Z grams of butter, I'll get the perfect amount per 1 tablespoon.'

That's a rough way to estimate dosage because it assumes that the maximum amount of THC available was extracted from the cannabis and that all of it got into the butter and was activated with 100 per cent efficiency. It's a calculation that works only to determine the ceiling – in other words, it is the absolute most THC you can possibly get. In reality, you're reducing potency at every step of the process, as cannabinoids are lost or destroyed.

Calculating Potency of Homemade Infusions

According to our cannabis lab, the THCA present in cannabis converts to THC at a rate of 0.88 per cent. Then, we have to consider the efficiency of our infusion method, which can vary from 40 to 60 per cent when you're infusing cannabis flower into butter or oil. Infusions are inefficient because some THC gets vaporised in the process and some is lost in the straining, remaining in the plant material. Also, different types of fat absorb cannabis at different rates, so an oil rich in saturated fats (such as coconut oil) tends to be the most effective for infusion. On the show, cannabis expert Ry Prichard uses a 0.7 per cent conversion rate to estimate the THC content of infusions. He says, 'Since we aren't able to determine the effectiveness of the fat infusion, we use this estimate as the ceiling.'

The next consideration is that baking or cooking with your cannabis-infused fat continues to convert acidic cannabinoid molecules to active forms, as some other THC molecules are evaporated at high temperatures. If you were to lab test your completed edibles, you would usually find that some THCA remains, meaning that some molecules evaded being decarboxylated – yet another blow to the potency of your finished dish.

So, it's complicated. With this disclaimer in mind, working with cannabis at home means that you need to be open to the possibility that you might eat a little more or less THC than planned on.

Vanessa Says: A lot of thought goes into serving size when finding the right dose. For example, a salsa is a great way to increase potency in increments, much as you do with spice preferences. It's a good starting analogy for people to find their sweet spot. If a dish is something you know people will chow down on, then a lighter dose or non-psychoactive CBD is best. Sometimes it's fun to use weed as a flavour element, even if it doesn't get you high. When Cat Cora visited the show, we had a lot of fun cooking up the leaves. They're tasty fried, candied or even chopped up into a quick salsa verde.

THC Dosing for the Home Cook

The two big questions when you're dosing: (1) How big is a serving? (2) How much THC should each serving contain?

Working backwards, you can determine that if you're baking a dozen cupcakes, and you think each guest will eat one, and your guests are newish to eating weed, you might aim for a dose of 10 milligrams of THC per cupcake. That means you'll need 120 milligrams of THC in the form of weed-infused butter for adding to the cupcake batter.

Assume you get a conversion rate of 70 per cent when making your infused butter. The 120 milligrams of THC you need for the cupcake batter is 70 per cent of 171.5 milligrams total THCA (51.5 milligrams are lost or destroyed during the infusion process). If you have access to cannabis flower that lab tests at 15 per cent THCA, you'll

Conversion of THC in Decarboxylated Cannabis Flowers to THC Content of Infused Butter
Based on an infusion of 3 grams cannabis into 225 grams/8 ounces butter (estimated)

Amount of THC per 1 gram of decarboxylated cannabis flower	Amount of THC when multiplied by 3 grams of cannabis going into infusion	Amount of THC lost during infusion process (30 per cent)	Amount of THC infused into 225 grams (8 ounces) of butter	Amount of THC per 1 tablespoon butter
35mg	105mg	31.5mg	73.5mg	4.5mg
70mg	210mg	63mg	147mg	9.2mg
105mg	315mg	94.5mg	220.5mg	13.8mg
140mg	420mg	126mg	294mg	18.4mg

need 1.2 grams cannabis flower for infusing into the amount of butter called for in the cupcake recipe.

While your cupcakes are baking, a small amount of THC will be lost due to oven heat. But you can still estimate that each cupcake will have at most 10 milligrams THC, and not worry if that estimate proves a little high.

In the recipes in this book, we've used lab-tested infusions, so we're able to get into the ballpark of dosing THC correctly. But variations will exist because of the potency of your starting material. We used Forbidden Fruit cannabis flower that tested at 9.05 per cent THC and Forbidden Fruit trim that tested at 3.68 per cent THC in their cured forms before being decarboxylated. Your weed might be more or less potent. We chose this strain because we wanted to keep the dosing low per serving.

Conversion of THCA in Cannabis Flowers
to Decarboxylated THC Content
Based on 1 gram cannabis (estimated)

Percentage of THCA per 1 gram of cannabis flower	THC in milligrams per 1 gram after decarboxylation
5	35
10	70
15	105
20	140

DO THE MATHS

Following these steps will help you estimate the THC content of your infusions.

1. Starting with lab-tested cannabis that comes with a THCA percentage, determine the remaining THC content in milligrams per 1 gram after decarboxylation, assuming a 70 per cent conversion rate of THCA to THC.

2. Multiply the THC content by however many grams of cannabis you are using to make your infusion. For example, we used 3 grams.

3. Subtract 30 per cent of the total THC, assuming that is the amount lost during the infusion process. The remaining THC is the total estimated amount present in the infusion.

4. Divide the total amount of THC by the number of tablespoons of butter used (16 tablespoons in our example) to determine the estimated amount of THC in milligrams per 1 tablespoon of the infusion.

Flavours

Cooking with cannabis is about more than getting high – there's a world of flavour to explore as well. Here's what you need to know to pair cannabis strains with different foods based on how they taste and smell.

Understanding Terpenes

If you hang out with people who are seriously into dabbing, you're likely to hear the word terpene, or terp for short – a lot. It's evolved into slang for anything that tastes flavourful or awesome. The obsession with terpenes happened as cannabis connoisseurs shifted from focusing solely on potency as the primary consideration to seeing taste and aroma in a more central role – echoing the world of fine wine and craft beer. After all, any halfway decent sample of cannabis will get you high, but not every bud tastes like a ripe Meyer lemon or smells like a pine forest.

Also, cannabis strains often used to be bred exclusively by growers looking for mind-melting psychoactivity. But it turns out that when given options, many of us actually prefer a less intense high. Weed with THC levels at 25 per cent or more packs a powerful punch. But there are plenty of consumers who will actually choose a less potent strain with around 15 per cent THC if it has a fantastic citrus taste. This is similar to the world of fine wine, where oenophiles, rather than seeking out the bottle with the highest alcohol content, look for the wine that tastes great and complements their meal.

What all this means is that the focus has now moved away from getting as wasted as possible to a more refined appreciation of the plant's diverse range of flavours and aromas. This is great news for our purposes, as it means when approaching a recipe we can source specific strains of cannabis with terpene profiles that complement what we're making.

Vanessa Says: Whenever we use terpenes – the fragrant oils of cannabis varieties – they go into a cold dish. They are volatile at high temperatures, potent in flavour and are used much like any other culinary extract – sparingly.

What's a Terpene?

Terpenes are one of the major chemical constituents of essential oils. Scientifically known as isoprenoids, terpenes do more than just add amazing smells to cannabis. There's increasing evidence these small molecules work together with cannabinoids to increase the plant's overall healing potential, a phenomenon articulated by leading researcher Dr Ethan Russo as the 'entourage effect'.

Developing and preserving high levels of terpenes in cannabis depends on how the cannabis was cultivated and processed. The growing medium, the amount of time the plant spent flowering, and whether or not it was cured properly all have a profound effect on the finished product. In other words, strains start out from seed or clone with a fixed potential to develop certain terpenes, and then the growing conditions and curing method determine to what extent those potentialities are expressed. Terpenes are composed of oil and alcohol, so the more terpenes in a concentrate, the softer and more fluid it is, with extracts such as sauce (see page 22) appearing less viscous due to a high terpene content.

More than 60 per cent of the terpene content of a plant is lost during the drying process. This fact has led hash makers to seek out new proprietary methods of extraction that use frozen fresh cannabis, rather than dried cured flowers, as a starting ingredient. Called 'live resin', this school of extract artistry is focused on preserving as many terpenes as possible.

Working with the Flavour of Cannabis

Anyone who has ever popped the top on a jar of good weed knows the distinctive, pungent scent of cannabis – a combination of intensely floral, sour and fruity aromas that is wholly unique unto itself but with a million variations. For example, there's Zkittlez, a strain that smells like a trademarked fruity candy. Or Sour Diesel, which reminds you of a splash of spilled gasoline next to a cheese shop. There are even such grossly named strains as Cat Piss, redolent of a sharp tang of ammonia shoved under your nose.

For many years, cannabis cooks focused on covering up the taste of weed because most people don't enjoy the intense grassy flavour. However, greater availability of hash and extracts have made the green taste from chlorophyll much less pronounced and therefore more appealing, and two schools of thought have now emerged in regard to the taste of cannabis. Some people still prefer not to have even a hint of cannabis flavour, especially when adding a psychoactive spin to a delicate recipe or a basic ingredient such as butter or oil. Seeking to minimise flavour has led to new infusion techniques involving blanching, as well as to the development of tasteless, dehydrated, powdered forms of water-soluble THC and flavourless, terpene-free extractions, such as distillate, that are used by many edible manufacturers. In the other camp, you'll find those who acknowledge weed is an acquired taste but have come to enjoy when a high-quality cannabis ingredient is thoughtfully incorporated into a dish. A slight 'weed taste' is also a good way to remind yourself with every bite that 'Hey, you're gonna get high', which will hopefully prevent overindulgence. The access to products such as terpenes and high-terpene extracts gives chefs an entirely new pantry of flavour possibilities to pair or contrast with in interesting ways.

Working with the diverse flavours of cannabis strains, rather than seeking to cover them up, is also a product of having access to increasingly luxurious cannabis-based ingredients. The flavour of well-made hash is pleasant, earthy and deeply spicy, adding a rich flavour to dishes that actually elevates the finished product. Flowers, trim and leaves still often have a strong chlorophyll taste, but you can control it by preparing them in different ways, such as frying or steeping like tea.

Vanessa Says: When planning a cannabis dinner party, you have more variables to consider. A pre-dinner smokable is a fun way to break the ice. (Personally, I like a joint of Girl Scout Cookies.) A microdosed *amuse-bouche* (bite-sized hors d'œuvre) or any finger food is good for whetting the appetite. Usually there is a main starch, such as rice or pasta. People pile these dishes on their plate, so use a lighter dose, or, better yet, a CBD option. More potent sauces are fun because guests can add as they please. It's polite to offer several dosing options. For dessert, well, sweets are the OG edible.

How to Taste and Pair Food with Cannabis

On *Bong Appétit*, cannabis expert Ry Prichard works with the guest chefs to dose each of the recipes. When asked about guidelines on pairing weed with food, he says that, perhaps more than any other plant in existence, cannabis has a chameleon-like ability to present itself with almost any scent and flavour found in nature. Cannabis can smell uncannily like oranges or lemons, it can smell like flowers, it can smell like a dead skunk, it can even smell like lavender-thyme cookies dipped in gasoline. Really, the possibilities are endless thanks to its tendency for genetic variation and its incredibly high essential-oil content.

The way a particular cannabis strain smells is most heavily influenced by its genetics, with the mother and father plants each imparting their signature scent to the next generation in different combinations. If a breeder marries a sweet-smelling plant with a sharp, acrid-smelling one, the resulting seed plants will exist along a spectrum, with some being fully sweet, some being fully acrid, and every variation in between. So even within one 'strain', such as Super Silver Haze, you may see a wide diversity of smells and flavours, each presenting a unique opportunity to pair (or contrast) with food and beverage.

Cannabis flavours, like those found in wine, beer and food, are the result of molecules that react with your taste buds, nasal cavities and brain to produce taste sensations. In the case of cannabis, these are largely the result of terpenes and flavonoids, which are the aromatic essential oils that, along with the cannabinoids, fill the heads of the trichome glands covering the plant and providing its unique profile. Similarly, like the flavours found in wine, beer and food, it's useful to come up with terms to describe them. Sometimes when tasting cannabis, it's possible to pick up very distinct and specific essence notes (e.g., blueberry muffin, tennis-ball canister, lemon peel); other times, the flavours blend in such a harmonious way that it is more of a blanket category description; for example: herby, sharp, acrid, sweet, tangy, citrusy or floral. These umbrella terms help to categorise and describe strains, but within those categories you'll find a huge number of subtleties and new combinations of flavours that were never thought possible.

One of the most exciting elements of cannabis, in a culinary sense, is its ability to interface with food and drink in very interesting and powerful ways. Much like a dry, acidic, citrus-forward rosé is the perfect partner to a piece of seared fish, the uncanny citrus qualities of Tangie, for example, complement a ponzu-soaked piece of sashimi. Today's modern cannabis products, such as separated terpenes, can give you incredible versatility, creating a rich dining experience as aroma and flavour notes bounce back and forth. While you are able to impart some complementary or contrasting flavours with infusion methods that use lower heat (such as the jar method in chapter 1), or by adding terpenes directly to food, you can also have great success pairing cannabis flavours with food via smoked or vaporised cannabis, specifically high-terpene concentrates. And, unlike alcohol, cannabis' ability to bring the user up or down with its different effects gives it an additional layer of experience, so a cannabis sommelier can start a meal with an uplifting, bright variety and end it with a rich, relaxing one.

When planning a cannabis-pairing dinner, think about the strongest flavour elements in the food and try to play off of those. Often, the most intense element is not the main protein or starch but rather a sauce or herbal component of a dish that makes it unique. Try to think about contrasting flavours as much as complementary ones; it's not always about picking something that tastes similar or goes with the dish in a conventional sense. An intriguing pairing can surprise guests and make them appreciate both the food and the cannabis more than they would have either on its own. To help you get started with understanding the ways to pair and contrast with cannabis, following are some of the most common scent and flavour categories that you'll come across.

Acrid

One function of terpenes is to deter predators from eating or otherwise damaging the plants. To do this, sometimes certain varieties will emit a smell that can be described as foul or overwhelming. Over the last decade, connoisseurs have tended to seek out these varieties, with the incredibly pungent, sharp scents cutting right through the overmatched plastic bag or jar attempting to keep them at bay. Known as 'gassy' or 'sour', these flavours can include elements of kerosene, glue, skunk, tyres, rubber and bad breath. While smoking something that smells like the old tennis balls in your grandpa's loft may not seem like an activity you want to do, these varieties also tend to be some of the most potent and unique, often with hordes of fans obsessing over their subtle differences. Pairing a gassy strain can be difficult, but these tend to do best with dishes that will stand up to them, such as smoked meats and herb-forward sauces (think chimichurri), but they also go suspiciously well with coffee.

Some of the most notorious gassy, acrid varieties are Chemdog, Gorilla Glue, Headband, any OG Kush variety, Sour Diesel and Triangle Kush.

Citrusy

While other flavour categories often have hints of citrus in the mix, there are some strains that have such a strong and uncanny citrus aroma that it's at times hard to distinguish them from the real thing. The presence of limonene (which is found in grapefruit, lime and lemon oils) is generally the reason a strain smells citrusy, but whether they smell like sweet lemon sherbet or garlic and lemon depends on the specific ratio and combination of other terpenes present. Citrusy varieties tend to be mentally uplifting and physically invigorating just like limonene itself, which makes sense because you more commonly find citrus-heavy flavours in strains that have traditionally been described as sativa. To pair most effectively with citrus varieties, think about how you'd use citrus in cooking; it's usually best to help brighten up a dish or add a lasting aftertaste that lingers on the palate.

Some varietals that exhibit a citrus-dominant aroma and flavour are Grapefruit, Jack's Cleaner, Jilly Bean, Lemon Diesel, Lemon G-13, Lemon Tree, Orange Cookies, Papaya, Soma's New York City Diesel (NYCD) and Tangie.

Vanessa Says: In the kitchen, we follow our nose. If a variety has more pronounced lemon notes, it might work well with fish or in a shortbread biscuit. That's where the culinary side of cooking with cannabis comes in. As far as what guests choose to smoke, that's personal preference.

Earthy

Like some of the more complex and challenging wines of the world, cannabis has a whole host of rich, dank, earthy flavours present at times. Leather, smoke, coffee, soil, peat and vegetation are some of the terms used to describe such strains, which tend to have been categorised as indicas over time. These varieties are often relaxing or sleep-inducing, perhaps due in part to the presence of terpenes such as myrcene and beta-caryophyllene, both of which are thought to have anti-anxiety properties.

Some rich and earthy varieties include Bruce Banner, Bubba Kush, Deadhead OG, Deep Chunk, Girl Scout Cookies, Hindu Kush, LA Confidential, Master Kush, Sour Bubble and Sunset Sherbert.

Floral

Cannabis is a flower after all, so it's expected that some varieties simply smell light and fragrant like other flowers. While certain strains kick down the door to your brain like a sensory SWAT team, others lightly dance in – calming and tranquil, blending in rather than taking over. One terpene that is very common in floral varieties is linalool, which is also the most common terpene, found in lavender and many other botanicals such as bay, coriander and sweet basil. These strains can range from very soft, pleasing scents to slightly more complex, grassy ones. Floral aromas are great to use in dishes such as subtly flavoured baked goods and to scent sauces and drizzles in unobtrusive ways.

Floral varieties of cannabis include Blackberry Kush, DJ Short's Flo, Grape Ape, Grape Stomper, Lavender, Purple Urkle, Strawberry Cough and UK Cheese.

Herbal

The general flavour present in cannabis can be described as 'herbal'. Though this admittedly covers a huge variety of scents, they are similar in that they can be found in other herbs such as rosemary, sage and eucalyptus, and also in things like pine trees. The most common terpenes in herbal varieties tend to be alpha-pinene, beta-pinene, beta-caryophyllene, humulene and terpinolene, the combination of which can cover the spectrum from the tangy citrus spice of a Jack Herer to the pine-forward floral sweetness of a Maui.

Common herbal varieties include Blue Dream, Jack Herer, Malawi, Mango Haze, Maui, S.A.G.E., Super Silver Haze and Trainwreck.

Sweet and/or Fruity

The first time you smell weed that is truly sweet, it's a life-changer. Since the odour that most casual users associate with cannabis is along the acrid, skunky side of things (because that's the way smoke usually smells), they're often totally surprised to find aromas ranging from lemon drops to candy floss to green papaya, or a combination of ten sweet things all rolled into one. Sweet varieties usually run a spectrum from the almost creamy, neutral sugary side to the tangy, tropical fruit side, all of which offer a lot of options when it comes to pairing. Though it's tempting to pair sweet with sweet, it is often more interesting to use the sweet strains as a way to cut through something acidic or to enhance something herbal. If a strain has the distinct qualities of a specific fruit, sometimes the flavour will come through clearly enough to replace the actual fruit in a recipe, similarly to the way you can use a fruit extract.

Common strains that fit into this category include Banana Kush, Blueberry, Bubblegum, Cinderella 99, Island Sweet Skunk, Lemon Skunk, Purple Urkle, Super Lemon Haze, Vanilla Kush and Zkittlez.

Working with Cannabis Flavours

Traditionally, most chefs of edibles have tried to hide or disguise the flavours of cannabis rather than accentuate them. While some of the subtleties of an individual strain are certainly lost during the decarboxylation and infusion processes, using lower heat (and/or less time) and utilising more gentle methods, such as the jar method, can allow the strain's flavour to express itself more clearly in the final product. In general, the lower the heat and the less time exposed to that heat, the more terpenes and flavour are preserved. Another tip is allowing infusion mixtures to cool before opening the jar; this allows the volatile scent molecules to recondense and stay in the infusion rather than flying out at the first chance.

If you're lucky enough to have access to cannabis terpenes, they are the absolute best way to give strain-specific flavour to dishes because they come with none of the bitter or harsh flavours that can result from using other products. Putting just a single drop of quality terpenes in the bottom of a flute glass and topping with champagne will totally change the aroma and flavour of the champagne. Stirring two drops into a béchamel sauce as it cools can take its neutral creamy flavour to an entirely new place. Terpenes and other high-flavour concentrates are giving chefs a fresh toolbox of flavour possibilities that did not exist even five years ago.

Terpenes

The primary reason cannabis strains smell and taste the way they do is because of terpenes, aromatic hydrocarbons (meaning they contain only hydrogen and carbon) found in virtually every plant species. Cannabis is special because it not only carries a high concentration of terpenes in its essential oils but it also contains a very wide variety of terpenes (more than one hundred) compared to most other plants. When you smell a certain strain of weed and it reminds you of pine or lemon, it's because your nose is absorbing many of the exact same molecules as it would when smelling those things. Though certain strains are high in limonene, for example, that doesn't mean limonene is the only thing contributing to their scent – each strain is a very complex fingerprint of terpenes that enhance, balance and cancel one another out, making it difficult at times to pinpoint what exactly you are smelling.

Beyond just smelling good (or bad), terpenes have definable physical and cerebral effects on humans, as demonstrated in ancient practices such as aromatherapy. For example, studies have shown that humans exposed to high limonene scents, such as grapefruit essential oil, often see improvement with depression, fatigue and headaches. Now, many modern cannabis researchers believe that the complex ratios of the cannabinoids and the aroma and flavour compounds, such as the terpenes and flavonoids that exist within a strain, are what actually produces its unique effects.

So smelling that bright, tangy Durban Poison makes you happy not only because you're about to smoke it soon and get really high but the actual compounds within it help cause that reaction. In addition, the way that an individual plant is grown can increase the amount of total terpenes as well as the presence of specific ones. This means that a skilled grower using a particular type of nutrient may bring out more of the strain-centric flavour and effect of a varietal than someone who just threw a seed in the ground and fed it water. Similarly, high-terpene concentrates may provide a more directed experience than flowers and terpene-free concentrates, such as distillate and isolate, thanks to the higher amounts of these compounds. To help understand terpenes further, here is a description of the most common ones and some popular varieties of cannabis in which they can be found.

Limonene

Present predominately in sativa strains, limonene also appears in citrus rinds, rosemary, juniper and peppermint and is a significant component of citrus-based cleaning products. Strains of cannabis that possess a bright, acidic, sweet lemon flavour are easily infused into butter or olive oil and paired with any sweet or savoury dish that traditionally uses lemons. Determine whether your chosen cannabis is more sweet, sour or tart and then pair accordingly. For example, Super Lemon Haze is a sativa that's more tart, perfect for pairing with a light sugary dessert, while a sweet Tangie would complement fish more readily, and a distinctive Sour Diesel will shine through even when paired with bold rosemary and rich lamb.

Look for Bubba Kush, Durban Poison, LA Confidential, Sour Diesel, Super Lemon Haze and Tangie, among many others.

Linalool

Floral and spicy, linalool is found in hundreds of plants, including lavender, sweet basil, mint, laurels, birch, rosewood and coriander, and has sedative, anti-anxiety and stress-relieving effects. For thousands of years, lavender has been considered an effective sleep aid due to the linalool it contains. The strain Lavender is rich in linalool, works well in desserts like cake and ice cream, and can be combined with lemon to create sophisticated cocktails or elixirs.

Found in Amnesia Haze, G-13, Headband, Ingrid, LA Confidential, Lavender and Skywalker OG, among others.

Myrcene

Present in hops, lemongrass, citrus, mangoes, verbena, bay leaves, ylang-ylang, eucalyptus and thyme, myrcene is earthy and musky and carries a hint of clove, balsamic and fruitiness. When creating an infusion with a myrcene-rich cannabis strain, consider the season, the mood of the occasion and the cuisine you'd like to cook. Citrus, mango, chillies and coconut milk work well with strains that express fruity or lemongrass terps, such as Pineapple Kush and Grand Daddy Purps. But other earthier myrcene-rich strains such as Northern Lights would pair better with richer flavours, including roasted meats, orange glazes, thyme and goat's cheese.

Found in Blue Dream, Himalayan Gold, Skunk #1, Sour Diesel and White Widow, among many others.

Pinene

The most common terp found in cannabis, pinene is also present in conifers like pine and fir trees, as well as herbs such as rosemary, basil, parsley, dill and sage, and is a principal component of turpentine. When using a cannabis strain high in pinene, such as Jack Herer or Island Sweet Skunk, infuse it into olive oil for a seamless integration into Mediterranean cuisine, and blend it with savoury, herbaceous flavours that complement the natural taste of weed. The strong flavours of grilled meats and vegetables, garlic and tomatoes stand up to an assertive addition of cannabis, while the richness of foods like egg yolk, mashed potatoes and duck provide a pleasant contrast to the herb.

Found in Bubba Kush, Chemdog, Dutch Treat, Island Sweet Skunk, Jack Herer, OG Kush, Romulan, Super Silver Haze and Trainwreck, among many others.

Preparing Your Weed for Cooking: Tips and Techniques

For many years, the sole goal of cooking with cannabis was to get as high as possible as efficiently as possible. Underground edibles makers traditionally focused on using less-pricey parts of the plant that aren't suitable for smoking and would otherwise go to waste, like the sugar leaves, trim, shake from the bottom of a bag, or low-quality schwag buds. Recipes from that era prioritised wringing every last particle of THC from these lesser cuts, with flavour a distant secondary consideration. So if you've ever wondered why pot food has a reputation for tasting pretty crappy, that's the reason.

In general, the more expensive a cannabis ingredient is, the better it will taste. Trim is cheap and tastes very green. Flower costs more and tastes better while still being herbaceous and vegetal, much like basil, rocket or parsley. Precious kief, hashes and extracts are pricier than flower and trim, but the absence of chlorophyll makes concentrates taste much better, with unique earthy, spicy flavours.

Today, with legalisation in many US states changing the game, weed costs are falling while the diversity of cannabis ingredients available – a dizzying array of extracts, hashes and flowers – is increasing exponentially. In the future, once the costs have dropped enough to make these concentrated ingredients accessible to nearly everyone, cooks will probably use kief and hash. You can eliminate the grassy taste of cannabis entirely by making your own kief, but you'll need a lot of weed to end up with even a little bit of the precious result. Yield is highly dependent on how resinous and full of trichomes the plant material is, so only a rough guesstimate is possible. If you use trim to make kief, you might yield 10 per cent of the weight of the plant matter, and if you use flower, the yield might be up to 20 per cent. For example, 450 grams (1 pound) of trim could be sifted to yield 45 grams of kief, while 450 grams (1 pound) of flower would be more resinous, yielding maybe 90 grams of kief.

It's easy to add a measured high to any dish if using kief. For example, 1 gram of the raw Forbidden Fruit kief we used for this book contains 44.5 milligrams of THC, enough to dose more than eight servings with 5 milligrams each. For a visual, that same gram of kief equals 1 teaspoon, so ⅛ teaspoon raw kief is sufficient to add a subtle psychoactive effect to a plate of food. Once you toast kief – decarboxylating it – that potency skyrockets, as acidic THCA converts into psychoactive THC, but the flavour will change to a much more pungent, roasted taste, losing most of its terpenes. Our raw Forbidden Fruit kief contained 4.5 per cent THC but also 58.4 per cent THCA, so when fully activated, it can reach up to 500 milligrams of THC per 1 gram of kief. That ⅛ teaspoon kief could now contain up to 62.5 milligrams of fully decarboxylated THC.

Making Kief

Sifting your herb through a kief box that collects THC-laden trichomes as you break up and roll your bud is a great way to passively bank some THC for a rainy day. Or, you can process your herb in a weed grinder with a kief-sorting compartment that will isolate the resin glands as you grind. With either of these methods, however, it'll take time to accumulate a decent amount of kief, which can then be sprinkled on top of a bowl, rolled into a joint or added to recipes much like a spice. To collect larger amounts of kief quickly, you can make a dry-ice shaker (see page 59, or buy one, if you're fancy) to separate the trichomes from the plant matter.

How to Activate THC Through Decarboxylation

Fresh-picked cannabis won't get you high if you eat it because the non-psychoactive THCA found naturally in the plant has to be heated before it transforms into the version of THC that very much does get you high. This happens instantly when you smoke a joint, and over a longer period of time when you activate cannabis before infusing it into food.

Also known as decarboxylating in chemistry terms, this process simply means removing the carboxyl molecule found in THCA (the non-psychoactive acidic form), thereby transforming it into the fun kind of THC. You can decarboxylate cannabis a few different ways, including quickly at a high temperature or slowly at a low temperature. 'Low and slow' has been the traditional favourite, as it minimises the risk of burning your precious pot. Keep in mind that THC boils off at 157°C/314°F, so you should never come close to that danger point. Terpenes are even more volatile, with delicate caryophyllene evaporating at 119°C/246°F, tougher linalool at 198°C/388°F, and other well-known terps disappearing at points in between.

Preserving as many cannabinoids and terpenes as possible means using a low temperature, with 120°C/240°F generally recommended for proper decarboxylation. Timing is also important, with 30 to 60 minutes typically recommended for a successful decarb. Remember, heating your cannabis for too long will result in THC converting to CBN, leaving you less high and much sleepier. Plant material with a higher moisture content will need longer to decarb than kief or hash, so keep that in mind when using an extract or hash for cooking. And if you are pressed for time, you can crank up the temperature to 150°C/300°F and toast (bake) the plant material for 10 to 15 minutes, though you'll be losing more terpenes.

Here, we describe two different methods for decarboxylation, baking (aka toasting) and one directly inspired by sous vide cooking, in which food enclosed in a vacuum-sealed bag is immersed in a hot water bath to cook at a precise, continuous temperature for a specific amount of time. You can pick the one that best fits your time, equipment, skill level and taste preferences. You can eat your properly decarboxylated cannabis as is (and it will get you high), combine it with a bit of melted butter or coconut oil and put into capsules, or infuse it into a basic ingredient such as butter, cream, milk, coconut oil, alcohol or glycerine. Always begin by coarsely grinding your cannabis material to increase its surface area.

Method 1: Baking

This method is simple, but be aware that many ovens can fluctuate wildly in temperature. So before you begin, use an oven thermometer to make sure your oven is properly calibrated.

Heat the oven to 100°C fan/120°C/240°F/gas ½.

Spread the freshly ground cannabis flower, trim, kief or hash on a glass pie plate in an even layer and cover the plate with aluminium foil, crimping the foil around the rim to seal securely.

If your cannabis is very dry or there's not much of it, toast for 30 minutes. If the flower or trim is green and moist or if you have more than 28 grams, toast for up to 60 minutes, checking and stirring it periodically to make sure it's not getting too brown or burned. The flowers should look toasted and smell very fragrant. If using kief or hash and working with no more than 14 grams, toast for 20 to 30 minutes. If processing more than 14 grams, toast for 45 to 60 minutes, stirring every 10 to 15 minutes, until it smells very toasty. When the kief or hash is done decarbing, it will be slightly browner than it was originally.

When the time is up, remove the pie plate from the oven and let it sit, covered, until it is cool to the touch. This step allows any vaporised cannabinoids to settle back into the plant matter. Use immediately, or transfer to an airtight glass container and store in a cool, dark place for up to 1 month.

This method can also make your weed taste toasted, which can work in some recipes but not in others.

Method 2: 'Sous Vide'

Sous vide cooking is a fairly recent culinary trend in which food enclosed in a vacuum-sealed bag is immersed in a hot water bath to cook at a precise, continuous temperature for a specific amount of time. This technology is tailor-made for infusing cannabis, which requires precise temperature control to maximise the THC extraction but control the bitter flavours that can come from over-extraction. You will need an immersion circulator and, ideally, a vacuum sealer to try this method. With this method, there's not really a way to over-extract the material, so you could 'set it and forget it' if you don't have 6 hours to sit by the stove.

To decarboxylate flowers, trim, kief or hash: Vacuum seal your cannabis ingredients in a food-safe plastic bag.

Set your sous vide cooker to 100°C/200°F.

Immerse the sealed bag in the hot water and allow it to simmer for 4 to 6 hours. Simmer longer for larger quantities.

To make infusions: In a food-safe plastic bag, combine decarboxylated cannabis with melted butter, oil or glycerine.

Vacuum seal the bag, immerse in the hot water, and allow it to simmer for 4 to 6 hours. Simmer longer for larger quantities.

Whether you choose to add that extra toasting step really depends on how high you want to get. If you're looking for a low dose, you can skip it. If you want to get as high as possible, definitely do it and then go directly to infusing your weed into a chosen fat, as decarboxylation before infusing is still the best way to fully activate all of the potential THC. If you want to rely on the heat of infusion to activate the THC, that's fine. It's just not as efficient.

IS DECARBOXYLATION NECESSARY?

Decarboxylation of cannabis is necessary if you want to get really fucking high. If you don't mind using more weed to get less high, you can skip the whole process and activate the THC in your cannabis during the infusion process. The results will still be psychoactive, but there will be significant unconverted THCA remaining in the herb, so it won't be as psychoactive as it could be.

Comparison of Decarboxylation on active THC Content of Cannabis Ingredients (Flower and Trim)

Type of Cannabis Ingredient	Time in a 120°C/ 240°F oven	THC Percentage by Weight	THC Content	Acidic THC Content
Flower: Forbidden Fruit strain (dried and cured)	30 minutes	10.89	34.9mg/g	84.2mg/g
	60 minutes	10.75	80.3mg/g	31mg/g
Trim: Forbidden Fruit strain (dried and cured)	30 minutes	7.69	72.3mg/g	5.3mg/g
	60 minutes	6.25	61.7mg/g	0.9mg/g

As you can see, 60 minutes at 120°C/240°F is plenty of time to activate almost all of the THCA in your flower or trim and convert it to THC. The THC percentage does begin to drop, however, because some cannabinoids are evaporating.

DRYING AND CURING CANNABIS

If you grow your own backyard cannabis plants, harvest them when the flowers are at their fullest and the trichomes, when examined under a magnifying glass, have turned from clear to a milky white. At this point, remove the fan leaves for juicing, cooking or compost. Hang the cut flower stalks upside down in a cool, dry, dark place until they are dry and the stems can be snapped, about 4 to 5 days.

The next step is to break down the plants into smaller pieces. Using a pair of small, sharp scissors, cut the flowers off the stalks and into smaller bundles of buds, removing as many stems and sugar leaves as possible. Reserve the trim for culinary purposes.

Cure the dry buds by packing them into glass canning jars and sealing for another 5 to 7 days. Uncap the jars every day and let them sit open for an hour or so, then seal again. This process allows any remaining moisture to slowly evaporate.

Test a flower after 5 days to check if it's properly cured. It should grind easily, roll nicely into a joint, and burn without going out or needing to be re-lit more than once, leaving behind a white ash. If the flowers are still too wet, continue curing for a few more days before checking again.

Of course, if you're buying flower at a dispensary, all of these steps have been handled for you.

DIY Kief Shaker

After shaking out the kief, you'll still need to toast it to make it much more psychoactive. Once you've done that, it's the perfect add-in to whatever you're planning on cooking. Just like cannabis flower or trim, kief is a raw plant ingredient that needs to be heated to fully activate all the potential THC. And if you happen to have frozen your freshly harvested plants, this kief is a great way to preserve more terpenes and flavours.

Equipment

Clean 950-ml/32-fl oz/4-cup canning jar

450ml/16fl oz/2 cups dry ice (if using dried cannabis)

2 or 3 rubber bands

30-cm/12-inch-square silk screen, 90 to 120 micron

30 x 40-cm/12 x 16-inch sheet of baking parchment

Small opaque glass jar with a tight lid

Metal dough scraper

7 grams trim or flower, dried and cured (see opposite) or frozen

Put the trim or flower in the canning jar; if using dried cannabis, add the dry ice. Use the rubber bands to secure the silk screen over the mouth of the jar.

Invert the jar over the baking parchment. Shake the jar vigorously to release the kief, which will be a golden blonde to tan powder, onto the paper. Stop shaking when the kief begins to show a slight green tinge. (This indicates the plant matter is beginning to break up and get into your kief.)

Transfer the kief from the parchment to the opaque jar, using the dough scraper to ease any bits still clinging to the screen into the jar. Cap the jar tightly. Store in a cool, dark place for up to 1 month (for maximum freshness) or freeze for up to 1 year.

Infusions

There are many different methods for infusing cannabis into fats, suitable for every skill level and tailored to fit various equipment modalities. But they all seek to accomplish the same goal: removing cannabinoids from the plant matter and transferring those precious molecules as efficiently as possible into the chosen fat.

Why Fats?

Cannabinoids are hydrophobic, meaning they hate water. But they have a fetish for lipids, gravitating towards fats whenever possible. For this reason, the most effective cannabis infusions use fats, including butter, oil, lard, schmaltz (clarified chicken or goose fat), cream and milk. Absorbing cannabis into your body along with fat also makes it more bioavailable, meaning it feels more potent in your body, versus eating the same amount of decarboxylated cannabis without the accompanying fat.

When it comes to the best fats to use, saturated fats that are solid at room temperature – butter, coconut oil, lard – seem to absorb more cannabinoids than liquid fats, such as oils, though the difference is negligible. Butter, oil, pancetta fat, double cream, cow's milk and coconut milk all work to get THC into food. Adding sugar has the effect of making THC seem more potent, hence the longtime association of weed food with sweets.

On their own, sugar and glycerine aren't great mediums for infusions, which is why we infuse cannabis into fat before combining it with honey. Alcohol does a good job of attracting cannabinoids and preserving them, but it's not as good as fat.

On the show, when Ry seeks to introduce cannabinoids to recipes that don't call for fat, he turns to modern extracts like activated isolates and distillates, as they dissolve easily into foods. Relatively new to the marketplace is water-soluble THC, a product of chemical tweaking that is primarily used for adding cannabis to products like drinks.

Vanessa Says: Hands down, my favourite part of throwing a cannabis dinner party is cooking up new ideas in the kitchen. Any dish can have cannabis in it as long as there is fat or alcohol. The challenge is to come up with new techniques. When Debbie Michail cold-smoked labneh, or Louis Tikaram smashed fried cannabis nugs into his Thai dressing, sparks went off. I remember the first time I tasted a cannabis fan leaf and thought, 'Yum! This tastes like shiso!'

Squeezing all the infused oil out of the plant matter improves your yield.

Weed-Infused Oil

MUNCHIES Test Kitchen

Makes 185ml/6fl oz/¾ cup

	THC IN MILLIGRAMS	
	Flower-Infused Oil	Kief-Infused Oil
1 tsp	3.5	2.8
1 tbsp	10.4	8.4
60ml/2fl oz/¼ cup	41.6	33.6
125ml/4fl oz/½ cup	83.2	67.2
185ml/6fl oz/¾ cup	124.8	100

This is the simplest, easiest way to get weed into food and then into yourself. It's a neat and clean method of infusing different oils simultaneously. Plus, it keeps the smells contained, for those of you with less-chill neighbours.

You can infuse cannabis into any type of oil. We typically use infused olive oil in salad dressings, marinades and salsas; our infused canola is in a dipping sauce that accompanies the Pork Wontons (see page 108); and infused coconut oil goes into the Strawberry 'Cheesecake' on page 205 and the whipped honey on page 74.

Infusing raw kief into olive oil won't return the most potent oil, but the oil will be subtle and nicely flavoured, making it appropriate for use in recipes where simple flavours would be overwhelmed by a grassy cannabis taste. Drizzle it over fresh pasta or the focaccia on page 223. Use a flower-infused olive oil for the tomato salad on page 120 or the panzanella-inspired salad on page 123, where the flavours complement the grassy taste of this oil, which is easy to dose at 10 milligrams THC per 1 tablespoon.

You can infuse a number of different oils simultaneously with this method, which keeps each oil in its own canning jar. (Label the top of each jar to avoid confusion.) If you are infusing coconut oil, you will need to melt it first, as it is solid at room temperature.

350-ml/12-fl oz canning jar
with lid

Stockpot

Tea towel

Silicone oven glove or jar tongs

Mesh strainer

Muslin

Liquid measuring jug

240ml/8fl oz/1 cup oil, such as
olive, coconut, grapeseed or
canola

3 grams cannabis flower or
1 gram raw kief

Vanessa Says: For the basic
infusion of flower into fat, you'll
find plenty of information about
decarboxylation, or heating
cannabis to release carboxylic
acid and activate the flower
before infusing it into fat. I am
more concerned with how long
the flower is infused into fat. The
longer a plant is steeped in fat,
the more bitter green flavour will
be pulled.

Pour the oil into the canning jar. Add the cannabis material and stir to combine. Seal the jar tightly.

Stand the jar upright in the stockpot and add water until it is level with the top of the jar. Place the stockpot, uncovered, over a high heat and bring to a low boil. Leave to boil for 2 hours, checking the water every now and again and adding more as needed to maintain the original level. After the first hour, 'burp' the jar by unsealing the lid to release any pressure build-up and then recap it.

After 2 hours, lay the tea towel on a heatproof work surface. Using the oven glove, remove the jar from the water, set it on the towel and leave to cool until it can be handled. Then, while the oil is still liquid, line the strainer with the muslin and strain the oil into the measuring jug, squeezing any solids at the very end to extract all of the fat. Compost or discard the plant matter. If you used kief, there's no need to strain.

Use right away, or transfer to a clean jar and store in the fridge or freezer for up to 3 months.

Pro Tip: An infused oil made with kief will taste better than one made with flower. We used raw kief for this infusion. For a big potency boost, decarboxylate your kief by toasting in the oven at 100°C fan/120°C/ 240°F/gas ½ for 30 minutes before infusing.

Comparison of THC Content of Olive Oil Infused with Decarboxylated Flower and Raw Kief

Type of Cannabis Ingredient	Amount of Each Infusion Ingredient	Activated THC	THC Content	Acidic THC Content
Flower: Forbidden Fruit strain (toasted for 60 minutes to decarb)	3g flower in 240ml/8fl oz/ 1 cup olive oil	10.4mg per 1 tbsp	0.8mg/g 0.7mg/ml	0.3mg/g 0.3mg/ml
Kief: Forbidden Fruit strain (raw)	1g kief in 240ml/8fl oz/ 1 cup olive oil	8.4mg per 1 tbsp	0.6mg/g 0.6mg/ml	2.3mg/g 2.2mg/ml

Weed-Infused Butter

MUNCHIES Test Kitchen

Makes 170g/6oz/¾ cup

	THC IN MILLIGRAMS	
	Flower-Infused Butter	Kief-Infused Butter
1 tsp	5.5	2
1 tbsp	16.7	6
60g/2oz/¼ cup	66.8	24
115g/4oz/½ cup	133.6	48
170g/6oz/¾ cup	200	72

You use the same method to infuse butter that you use to infuse oil. For the most efficient infusion, purchase butter that has a higher butterfat content. We store the finished butter in a jar, but you can also freeze it in an ice-cube tray, which makes it easy to measure consistent doses.

Although the infusion process doesn't do much to activate the THC in kief, we find that butter infused with kief tastes the best, making it perfect for diners seeking a low THC dose with excellent flavour. It is ideal for simple applications that call for larger amounts of butter, such as drizzling over popcorn or spreading on a piece of toasted rustic bread. The flower-infused butter works well for baking, as it has relatively low potency and a pleasant but distinct cannabis flavour. Use it in the brownies for the sundae on page 195 or in the Adult Celebration Cake on page 211.

350ml/12fl oz canning jar with lid

Stockpot

Tea towel

Silicone oven glove or jar tongs

Mesh strainer

Muslin

Liquid measuring jug

225g/8oz/1 cup unsalted butter (with a high butterfat content), melted

3 grams cannabis flower or 1 gram raw kief

Pour the butter into the canning jar. Add the cannabis material and stir to combine. Seal the jar tightly.

Stand the jar upright in the stockpot and add water until it is level with the top of the jar. Place the stockpot, uncovered, over a high heat and bring to a gentle simmer. Leave to simmer for 2 hours, checking the water every now and again and adding more as needed to maintain the original level. Make sure it never reaches a full boil. After the first hour, 'burp' the jar by unsealing the lid to release any pressure build-up and then recap it.

After 2 hours, lay the tea towel on a heatproof work surface. Using the oven glove, remove the jar from the water, set it on the towel, and leave to cool until it can be handled. Then, while the butter is still liquid, line the strainer with the muslin and strain the butter into the measuring jug, squeezing any solids at the very end to extract all of the butter. Compost or discard the plant matter. If you used kief, you don't need to strain.

Use right away, or transfer to a clean jar and store in the fridge for up to 2 weeks or in the freezer for up to 3 months.

Comparison of THC Content of Butter Infused with Decarboxylated Flower and Raw Kief

Type of Cannabis Ingredient	Amount of Infusion Ingredients	Activated THC	THC Content	Acidic THC Content
Flower: Forbidden Fruit strain (toasted for 60 minutes to decarb)	3g flower in 225g/8oz/ 1 cup melted butter	16.7mg per 1 tbsp	1.2mg/g	0.5mg/g
Kief: Forbidden Fruit strain (raw)	1g kief in 225g/8oz/ 1 cup melted butter	6.1mg per 1 tbsp	0.4mg/g	2.9mg/g

Weed-Infused Brown Butter

MUNCHIES TEST KITCHEN

Makes 170g/6oz/¾ cup

0.5 gram raw kief

170g/6oz/¾ cup unsalted butter, cut into 1-tablespoon pieces

	THC IN MILLIGRAMS
1 tsp	2.9
1 tbsp	8.8
60g/2oz/¼ cup	35.2
115g/4oz/½ cup	70.4
170g/6oz/¾ cup	106

Nutty, toasty brown butter is good over the gnocchi on page 141 or in the chocolate chip cookies on page 196. Its earthy, umami flavour is only improved with the addition of raw kief. Making brown butter is easy, but you do have to pay attention so it doesn't burn, which would be a major bummer if you've already poured it over a bunch of kief.

Put the kief in a small heatproof bowl.

In a sauté pan over a medium heat, melt the butter, stirring constantly. The butter will melt, then begin to bubble and foam. When the foam starts to subside, the milk solids will begin to brown and the butter will smell nutty. Keep stirring for just a second, then pour the brown butter over the kief and stir to dissolve.

Let the butter cool and set before using, or transfer to a clean jar, leave to cool, cover and store in the fridge for up to 3 days or in the freezer for up to 6 months.

Pro Tip: You can increase the potency of this brown butter by decarboxylating the kief. Place it in a ramekin, cover the ramekin tightly with aluminium foil and toast in the oven at 100°C fan/120°C/240°F/ gas ½ for 15 minutes. We were surprised to see the weed-infused brown butter return a higher lab test result than regular infused butter – it's probably because the super-fast infusion preserves more cannabinoids.

Weed-Infused Coconut Milk

MUNCHIES Test Kitchen

Makes 240ml/8fl oz/1 cup

	THC IN MILLIGRAMS
1 tsp	1.9
1 tbsp	5.9
60ml/2fl oz/¼ cup	23.6
125ml/4fl oz/½ cup	47.2
185ml/6fl oz/¾ cup	70.8
240ml/8fl oz/1 cup	93.6

Equipment

Double boiler

Mesh strainer

Muslin

Liquid measuring jug

7 grams cannabis trim, ground and decarboxylated (see page 54)

240ml/8fl oz/1 cup coconut milk

Infusing coconut milk is a great option for vegan dishes, along with a variety of curries and Thai or Indian soups and stews. We used infused coconut milk in the seafood stew on page 183 and the crab gratin on page 114.

Set up the double boiler and bring the water to a simmer. Combine the trim and coconut milk in the top of the double boiler and cook, stirring occasionally, for 30 minutes. Remove from the heat and leave to cool.

Line the strainer with the muslin and strain the coconut milk into the measuring jug, squeezing the solids at the very end to extract all of the coconut milk. Compost or discard the plant matter.

Use right away, or transfer to a clean jar and store in the fridge for up to 4 days.

Weed-Infused Cream

MUNCHIES Test Kitchen

Makes 240ml/8fl oz/1 cup

Equipment

Double boiler

Mesh strainer

Muslin

Liquid measuring jug

7 grams cannabis trim,
ground and decarboxylated
(see page 54)

240ml/8fl oz/1 cup double cream

	THC IN MILLIGRAMS
1 tsp	11
1 tbsp	33.5
60ml/2fl oz/¼ cup	134
125ml/4fl oz/½ cup	268
185ml/6fl oz/¾ cup	402
240ml/8fl oz/1 cup	535

Always use the best organic, full-fat cream you can find so there are enough lipids to support a potent cannabis infusion. Non-dairy creams can also be infused using this method, especially coconut cream, which has a high fat content. For milk alternatives made from almond, hemp or soy, the fat content must be 4 grams (⅛ ounce) per serving, at the very least, or you're just wasting weed.

Use this infused cream to create the ricotta on page 233, the ice cream on page 193, the nacho sauce on page 99 or the filling for the Adult Celebration Cake on page 211.

Set up the double boiler and bring the water to a simmer. Combine the trim and cream in the top of the double boiler and cook, stirring occasionally, for 30 minutes. Remove from the heat and leave to cool.

Line the strainer with the muslin and strain the cream into the measuring jug, squeezing the solids at the very end to extract all of the cream. Compost or discard the plant matter.

Use right away, or transfer to a clean jar and store in the fridge for up to 4 days.

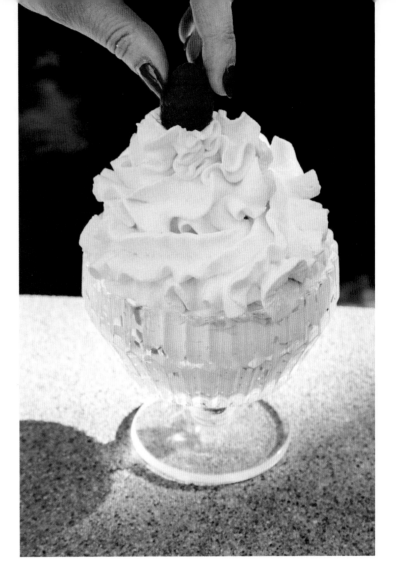

Whipped Weed-Infused Cream

60ml/2floz/¼ cup weed-infused cream (see opposite)

60ml/2floz/¼ cup double cream

1 tablespoon icing sugar

½ teaspoon vanilla extract

In a large bowl, combine the infused cream, double cream, icing sugar and vanilla. Using a whisk or handheld blender, beat until stiff peaks form. Keep refrigerated for up to 2 days; re-whip if it looks deflated.

Whipped Weed-Infused Honey or Syrup

MUNCHIES TEST KITCHEN

Makes 185ml/6fl oz/¾ cup

	THC IN MILLIGRAMS
1 tsp	1.5
1 tbsp	4.7
60ml/2fl oz/¼ cup	18.8
125ml/4fl oz/½ cup	37.6
185ml/6fl oz/¾ cup	56

Equipment

450-ml/16-fl oz canning jar with lid

Stockpot

Tea towel

Silicone oven glove or jar tongs

Blender

Squeezy bottle

185ml/6floz/¾ cup honey

2 tablespoons MCT coconut oil

0.5 gram kief

When you buy weed honey in an L.A. dispensary, chances are it's made by simply mixing a viscous cannabis concentrate extract directly into honey, resulting in a product with little bioavailability. This honey is simple to make, and it is effective because of the addition of oil as fat. It's important to use medium-chain triglycerides (MCT) oil, which is a type of coconut oil that is liquid at room temperature. Otherwise your honey will solidify at cooler temperatures and be difficult to pour.

Use this honey in the peanut butter on page 232 and in the Adult Celebration Cake on page 211. You can also stir it directly into a cup of tea or drizzle it over ice cream. This same method can be used with molasses, agave nectar or maple syrup.

Pour the honey and coconut oil into the canning jar, add the kief and stir to combine. Seal the jar tightly.

Stand the jar upright in the stockpot and add water until it is level with the top of the jar. Place the stockpot, uncovered, over a high heat and bring to the boil. Lower the heat and simmer for 2 hours, checking the water every now and again and adding more as needed to maintain the original level.

After 2 hours, lay the tea towel on a heatproof work surface. Using the oven glove, remove the jar from the water, set it on the towel and leave to cool until it can be handled. Then, pour the infused honey into the blender and blend on high speed until the mixture is emulsified, about 3 to 5 minutes.

Transfer the honey to the squeezy bottle for easy access and store in a cool, dark place for up to 6 months.

Nitrous Green Dragon

DON LEE

Makes 450ml/16fl oz/2 cups

	THC IN MILLIGRAMS
1 tsp	0.8
1 tbsp	2.5
60ml/2fl oz/¼ cup	10
125ml/4fl oz/½ cup	20
185ml/6fl oz/¾ cup	30
240ml/8fl oz/1 cup	40
450ml/16fl oz/2 cups	80

Equipment

0.5-litre/17-fl oz heat-tolerant whipped cream dispenser

Nitrous-oxide charger

2 x 450-ml/16-fl oz canning jars with lids

Stockpot

Tea towel

Silicone oven glove or jar tongs

Mesh strainer

Muslin

3 grams ground cannabis flower

450ml/16fl oz/2 cups mezcal

By using a nitrous oxide-powered whipped-cream dispenser to 'force infuse' cannabinoids into liquor, legendary New York City bartender Don Lee created a gorgeous, transparent emerald booze that actually tastes really good. This once-revolutionary method quickly became the favoured way to create basic ingredients for cannabinated cocktails, sparking a rush of interest from high-minded mixologists far and wide. There are other ways to infuse cannabis into alcohol that don't require a whipped-cream dispenser, but if you're serious about creating weed cocktails, this is the way to do it! It works for infusing any alcohol, from mezcal (called for here) to gin, whisky, brandy, tequila and more.

Put the cannabis material and mezcal in the canister of the whipped-cream dispenser. Screw on the dispenser head and charge with the nitrous-oxide charger according to the manufacturer's instructions. Let the canister sit for 5 minutes.

Vent out the pressurised gas. Stir the liquid and then let it sit for a minute, until the gas boils off. (At this point, the liquor will be imbued with cannabis flavour but won't have developed much THC potency. The next step decarboxylates the weed liquor, making it

continued

Nitrous Green Dragon, *continued*

potent as well as cannabis-flavoured.) Pour the mezcal-weed mixture into a canning jar and seal the top loosely.

Stand the jar upright in the stockpot and add water until it is level with the alcohol. Place the stockpot, uncovered, over a medium heat and bring to a simmer. Leave to simmer for 1 hour, checking the water every now and again and adding more as needed to maintain the original level.

After 1 hour, lay the tea towel on a heatproof work surface. Using the oven glove, remove the jar from the water, set it on the towel and leave to cool until it can be handled.

Line the strainer with the muslin and strain the mezcal into the second jar, squeezing the solids at the very end to extract all of the alcohol. Compost or discard the plant matter.

Store in a cool, dark place for up to 6 months. Use sparingly, as the combined effects of mezcal and cannabis are intense; the recommended serving size is just 45ml/1½fl oz/3 tablesoons in any cocktail.

INFUSING ALCOHOL

If you want to make cannabis cocktails, you can infuse weed into spirits and use the cannabinated liquors to create mind-bending concoctions. Most traditional recipes involve little more than steeping together alcohol and cannabis in a cool, dark place for several months. But crafty stoners recently figured out improvements to increase potency and speed production time by adding heat and/or pressure.

Traditionally, highly concentrated alcohol-based tinctures were used as folk remedies. These same tinctures can be diluted in drinks, replacing infused liquors, to create cannabis cocktails.

Using Everclear, a popular brand of high-proof grain alcohol, to create a tincture will yield the highest potency product. Unfortunately, it tastes awful and burns when dropped under the tongue, and is not all that easy to get hold of. Many commercially available tinctures trade out grain alcohol in favour of grape spirits distilled from wine, which are 85 per cent proof alcohol by volume compared to 95 per cent for Everclear. If you can't source this particular brand, aim for a neutral grain spirit with the highest ABV you can find.

Pro Tip: We made our infusions into alcohol with dried and cured flower that had not been decarboxylated because we wanted to preserve the cannabis flavour, but you could use decarb'ed flower to increase the psychoactivity of these drinks if desired.

Vanessa Says: Alcohol and cannabis are a tricky combo; we've infused gins and served wine on the show. Balance is key, but I think wine and cannabis can be a classic pairing. The terpenes, the terroir – they complement each other well. Also, there's an anecdotal theory that it is best to smoke then drink, rather than the other way around.

Everclear Cannabis Tincture

MUNCHIES TEST KITCHEN

Makes 125ml/4fl oz/½ cup

	THC IN MILLIGRAMS
1 tsp	14.3
1 tbsp	43
60ml/2fl oz/¼ cup	172
125ml/4fl oz/½ cup	344.3

Equipment

20-cm/8-inch round tempered-glass pie plate

Saucepan large enough to fit the pie plate on top snugly

Mesh strainer

Muslin

Liquid measuring jug

7 grams cannabis flower, ground and decarboxylated (see page 54)

1 x 375-ml/13-fl oz bottle Everclear or other high-proof grain alcohol

This basic recipe for a cannabis tincture can be used not only for making cocktails but also for the pepperoni recipe from chef Justin Severino on page 239. Don't go drinking this; the flavour is harsh and it's very potent.

On the pie plate, combine the cannabis flower and alcohol.

Half-fill the saucepan with water, set over a high heat and bring to the boil. Put the pie plate on top of the saucepan, turn the heat to medium and allow the alcohol to evaporate slowly until the liquid is reduced by half, about 45 to 60 minutes. Remove from the heat and leave to cool.

Line the strainer with the muslin and strain the alcohol into the measuring jug, squeezing the solids at the very end to extract all of the tincture. Compost or discard the plant matter.

Use right away, or transfer to a small clean jar, cap tightly and store in a cool, dark place for up to 6 months.

Pro Tip: Infusing flammable alcohol over a gas flame is dangerous; so be careful. If you can, use an electric burner; or at the very least, make sure you have plenty of ventilation.

Glycerine Cannabis Tincture

MUNCHIES TEST KITCHEN

Makes 240ml/8fl oz/1 cup

	THC IN MILLIGRAMS
1 tsp	13
1 tbsp	39
60ml/2fl oz/¼ cup	156
125ml/4fl oz/½ cup	312
240ml/8fl oz/1 cup	624

Equipment

450-ml/16-fl oz canning jar

Stockpot

Tea towel

Silicone oven glove or jar tongs

Mesh strainer

Muslin

Liquid measuring jug

240ml/8fl oz/1 cup organic food-grade glycerine

7 grams cannabis flower, ground and decarboxylated (see page 54)

This basic recipe for a glycerine-based cannabis tincture can be used to infuse cocktails, sauces and desserts; Forbidden Fruit flowers turned this one (pictured opposite, top left) deep purple. If you find yourself adding just small amounts of it to drinks or the like, store in a dark-coloured glass bottle with an eye dropper for ease of dosing.

Pour the glycerine into the canning jar. Add the cannabis flower and stir to mix. Seal the jar tightly.

Stand the jar upright in the stockpot and add water until it is level with the top of the jar. Place the stockpot, uncovered, over a high heat and bring to a low boil. Lower the heat and simmer for 2 hours, checking the water every now and again and adding more as needed to maintain the original level. After the first hour, 'burp' the jar by unsealing the lid to release any pressure build-up and then recap it.

After 2 hours, lay the tea towel on a heatproof work surface. Using the oven glove, remove the jar from the water, set it on the towel and leave to cool completely. Line the strainer with the muslin and strain the tincture into the measuring jug, squeezing any solids at the very end to extract all of the tincture. Compost or discard the plant matter.

Use right away, or transfer to a clean small jar and store in a cool, dark place for up to 6 months.

Drinks

Manhattan

MUNCHIES TEST KITCHEN

Makes 1 cocktail

30ml/1fl oz weed-infused whisky (see Nitrous Green Dragon, page 77)

15ml/½fl oz sweet vermouth

1 or 2 dashes Angostura bitters

Orange peel twist or maraschino cherry (Luxardo brand, if possible), to garnish

The herbal undertones of sweet vermouth get another layer of herb with infused whisky in this mellow version (pictured opposite, left) of a traditional drink, perfect for pairing with a cold night and a glowing fireplace. Infusing your whisky with a strong citrusy strain like Tangie would make this Manhattan extra-special.

Chill a coupe glass. Half-fill a mixing glass or a cocktail shaker with ice, add the whisky, vermouth and bitters and stir with a bar spoon for 20 to 30 seconds. Strain into the chilled glass and garnish with an orange twist or cherry before serving.

Dirty Martini

MUNCHIES TEST KITCHEN

Makes 1 cocktail

30ml/1fl oz gin

30ml/1fl oz weed-infused gin (see Nitrous Green Dragon, page 77)

7ml/¼fl oz/½ tablespoon dry vermouth

7ml/¼fl oz/½ tablespoon olive juice

Spanish olives, to garnish

Martinis are amazing because they're basically a socially sanctioned way to drink an entire glass of gin, by itself, in public. And if you're already going to do that, you may as well add some bud to it, too. A gassy strain such as Sour Diesel or OG Kush, or a pinene-rich weed like Bubba Kush, Trainwreck or Chemdog would complement the intense savoury flavours from the olive juice that make this martini (pictured opposite, right) so dirty.

Chill a martini glass. Half-fill a mixing glass or a cocktail shaker with ice, add both gins, the vermouth and olive juice and stir with a bar spoon for 20 to 30 seconds. Strain into the chilled glass and garnish with the olives before serving.

White Negroni

Daniel Nelson

Makes 1 cocktail

30ml/1fl oz weed-infused gin (see Nitrous Green Dragon, page 77)

30ml/1fl oz Cocchi Americano

30ml/1fl oz Herbal-Infused Vermouth (see below)

Orange peel twist, to garnish

Daniel Nelson, partner at The Black Cat on Los Angeles' Sunset Boulevard, is an OG marijuana mixologist and pioneer in the field. He's been making cocktails at weed dinners, both secret and open, for a long time, and was among the first bartenders to openly share his approach to mixing booze and weed. For this crystal-clear riff on a classic Negroni (pictured opposite, right), he uses vermouth infused with both lavender and cannabis (such as Lavender Haze or Amnesia Haze) to amp up the drink's floral and herbal notes. The usual Campari gets replaced with Cocchi Americano, a clear vermouth steeped with botanicals, including bitter cinchona bark and citrus peel.

For the infused vermouth, simmering the lavender releases terpenes into the mix, making for a reliable way to preserve flavours. This recipe doesn't add psychoactive THC to the liquor, but it will add weed flavour.

Combine the gin, Cocchi Americano and vermouth in a mixing glass and stir with a bar spoon. Pour over ice in a rocks glass and garnish with an orange twist before serving.

Herbal-Infused Vermouth

Makes 350ml/12fl oz/1½ cups

375ml/13fl oz dry vermouth

2 tablespoons fresh lavender flowers

1 gram favourite cannabis flower, freshly ground (optional)

In a small saucepan over a medium heat, combine the vermouth, lavender and cannabis flower and bring to a simmer. Let the liquid simmer for 3 minutes, then remove from the heat and leave to cool.

Line a strainer with muslin and strain the cooled vermouth into a measuring jug.

Use right away, or transfer to a bottle, cap tightly and store in the fridge for up to 3 weeks.

French 75

Makes 1 cocktail

30ml/1fl oz weed-infused gin
(see Nitrous Green Dragon,
page 77)

15ml/½fl oz freshly squeezed
lemon juice

2 dashes Sugar Syrup
(see below)

Champagne for topping

Lemon twist, to garnish

More like a French 420, amirite? An ultra-chill 5 milligrams of
THC make this classic sparkler (pictured on page 89, left) especially
celebratory without getting you too stoned. Infusing your gin with a
strain high in limonene, like Super Lemon Haze, brings this cocktail to
the next level.

Chill a champagne flute. Fill a cocktail shaker with ice, add the gin,
lemon juice and sugar syrup; cover and shake vigorously for 15 to
20 seconds. Strain into the chilled glass, top with Champagne and
garnish with a lemon twist before serving.

Sugar Syrup
Makes 240ml/8fl oz/1 cup

200g/7oz/1 cup sugar

240ml/8fl oz/1 cup water

In a small saucepan over a medium-high heat, combine the sugar
and water. Cook, stirring occasionally, until the sugar dissolves.
Remove from the heat and leave to cool completely before using.

Store in an airtight container in the fridge for up to 3 months.

THC
2.4mg per serving;
9.44mg total recipe

Sangria

MUNCHIES TEST KITCHEN

Makes 2 litres/70fl oz/8¾ cups (4 servings)

750ml/26floz (1 bottle) red wine

450ml/16fl oz/2 cups apple juice

60ml/2fl oz/¼ cup weed-infused brandy (see Nitrous Green Dragon, page 77)

60ml/2fl oz/¼ cup orange liqueur

2 tablespoons freshly squeezed lemon juice, plus 2 lemons, thinly sliced crossways

5 fresh strawberries, hulled and thinly sliced

4 small, sticky fresh cannabis flowers right off a plant

750ml/26floz/3¼ cups lemon-flavoured sparkling water

We got weed into this sangria (pictured on page 92, top) a couple of different ways. We dropped a few fresh, sticky buds straight off the plant into the wine and let it sit overnight, which got us started with a flavourful (but not psychoactive) base. If you're in this for the psychoactive properties, you'll want to up the ante a little with infused brandy. The higher alcohol content of brandy means it can absorb more THC, packing a significantly higher punch than wine. Use your favourite red wine blend for this; no need to sacrifice an expensive single varietal for sangria. (A few winemakers, like Pax Mahle at Wind Gap Wines in northern California, are currently making wine that gets bud folded in during the fermentation process so the end product is both flavoured and dosed. But those bottles are hard to come by. That said, if you can get weed wine and want to use it in this, we're definitely not going to stop you. Just be sure you figure in the higher dosage.)

In a large jug, combine the wine, apple juice, brandy, orange liqueur, lemon juice, sliced lemons, strawberries and cannabis flowers and stir well. Cover and refrigerate for at least 4 hours or preferably overnight. Stir in the sparkling water and serve in glasses over ice.

Margarita

Tim Hollingsworth

Makes 1 cocktail

8 cannabis leaves, each about 5cm/2 inches in diameter

45ml/1½fl oz weed-infused blanco tequila (see Nitrous Green Dragon, page 77)

20ml/¾fl oz/1½ tablespoons freshly squeezed lime juice

20ml/¾fl oz/1½ tablespoons grapefruit liqueur (such as Giffard Pamplemousse)

20ml/¾fl oz/1½ tablespoons Sugar Syrup (see page 90)

1 pinch kosher salt or coarse sea salt

2 thin slices fresh bird's-eye or other hot chilli

At his restaurant Otium in Los Angeles, Chef Tim Hollingsworth blends peppery nasturtium leaves into a hyper-green cocktail that he rounds out with grapefruit liqueur, hot bird's-eye chilli and infused blanco tequila. But for us, he swapped in cannabis leaves, which, while they're not psychoactive, add a grassy herbal backbone to this refreshing drink (pictured opposite, bottom). If you can't find cannabis or nasturtium in your backyard, you can use a little rocket.

In a blender, combine seven of the cannabis leaves, the tequila, lime juice, grapefruit liqueur, sugar syrup, salt and a chilli slice and blend on high speed for 10 seconds.

Fill a cocktail shaker with ice, pour in the blended mixture, cover and shake for 10 seconds, until the shaker ices over slightly.

Pour the contents over ice in a rocks glass and then garnish with the remaining cannabis leaf and chilli slice before serving.

THC

7.5mg per cocktail

With cannabis flower:
About 17.5mg

Apple Bong

DEVON TARBY

Makes 1 cocktail

1 large Red Delicious or
other red apple

½ lemon

45ml/1½fl oz weed-infused
mezcal (see Nitrous Green
Dragon, page 77)

30ml/1fl oz apple juice

15ml/½fl oz freshly squeezed
lemon juice

15ml/½fl oz Sugar Syrup
(see page 90)

1 drop XJ-13 terpenes (optional)

0.5 gram cannabis flower (such
as Jack Herer or XJ-13) for
smoking

Of course you know what an apple bong is. You're human after all,
and you probably also went to school. But cocktail-hero Devon Tarby
of L.A.'s Honeycut and The Normandie Club wants you to take apple
carving from a furtive dorm-room pursuit to a much more soigné
experience.

Here, an apple (the favourite of every teacher's pet) gets hollowed
out and filled with a cocktail built around smoky weed-infused
mezcal – Devon recommends Bruxo's Espadín – that gets even smokier
as you hit the bong. The smokiness of the mezcal pairs naturally with
cannabis flavours like XJ-13 or Jack Herer, a particularly good choice
for infusing the liquor as well as smoking through the apple pipe. Amp
up the flavours by adding a drop of XJ-13 terpenes to the cocktail if you
can get your hands on them. Sip a little, smoke a little, sip a little more.
Bong water never tasted so good.

Carefully cut off the top (stem end) of the apple and rub the exposed
flesh with the lemon half. Cover the top and put aside. Next, carve
out the apple flesh (eat or use for juice), creating a small bowl with
5-mm/¼-inch-thick sides for holding the drink. Rub the inside of the
apple with the lemon half, cover the apple bowl and put aside.

Fill a cocktail shaker with ice; add the mezcal, apple juice, lemon
juice, sugar syrup and terpenes (if using), cover and shake vigorously
for 15 to 20 seconds. Strain into the apple bowl (the whole cocktail
might not fit, so have a glass on the side in case there is extra).

Take a straight stiff straw and push it through one side of the
reserved apple top, then remove any flesh from the straw. Next, make
a small reservoir on the apple top. The hole should be big enough to
allow smoke to pull through, but not so large that your weed will
fall into the cocktail. Place the apple top back on the apple, put the
cannabis flower in the reservoir, and take a sip of the cocktail. Once
there is enough headroom inside the apple (about 5mm/¼ inch),
light the bowl. Enjoy your high and the smoky flavour of the rest of
the cocktail.

Appetisers

THC

4.2mg per serving;
16.7mg total recipe

With weed-infused cream:
12.6mg per serving;
50.2 total recipe

Sour Cream and Onion Nachos

MUNCHIES TEST KITCHEN

Serves 4

3 tablespoons unsalted butter

1 tablespoon flower-infused butter (see page 68)

680g/1lb 8oz onions, thinly sliced

435ml/15¼fl oz/1¾ cups double cream

1 tablespoon weed-infused cream (see page 72; optional)

125ml/4fl oz/½ cup soured cream

1 teaspoon garlic powder

1 teaspoon onion powder

Kosher salt or coarse sea salt

250g/9oz bag Kettle Chips

3 spring onions, white and tender green parts, thinly sliced

1 bunch chives, finely chopped

You can take chips and dip from our cold, dead hands. But still, you know what's better than chips and dip? Potato-chip nachos layered with caramelised onions and drizzled with warm, weed-laced sour cream sauce. You can either caramelise your onions in a little bit of flower-infused butter, or you can add weed-infused cream to the sour cream sauce – or both. Live large.

In a frying pan over a medium heat, melt both the butters. Add the onions and cook, stirring occasionally, for about 1 hour, until deeply golden and caramelised. Remove from the heat and keep warm.

In a saucepan over a medium heat, bring the double cream to a simmer. (If using the weed-infused cream, add it now.) Cook for about 15 minutes, until thickened and reduced by almost half. Stir in the soured cream, garlic powder and onion powder and season with salt, mixing the cream sauce well. Remove from the heat.

Spread the chips on a serving platter and top with the caramelised onions. Drizzle with the cream sauce and sprinkle with the spring onions and chives. Serve warm.

Vanessa Says: Add the infused cream for an extra THC boost. Using a variety rich in caryophyllene, such as OG Kush, will add a peppery note to the dish.

THC
4.7mg per pakora;
281.5mg total recipe

Red Beetroot Pakoras

Fatima Ali

Makes 60 pakoras

For the Goat's Cheese Sauce

50g/2oz/½ cup crumbled fresh goat's cheese

2 tablespoons plain Greek yogurt

1 teaspoon flower-infused olive oil (see page 64)

Juice of 1 orange

Kosher salt (or coarse sea salt) and freshly ground black pepper

For the Pakoras

2 tablespoons coriander seeds

1 tablespoon ground cumin

1 teaspoon chilli powder

0.5 gram raw kief

3 red beetroots, peeled and coarsely grated

375g/13oz/3 cups gram flour, plus more as needed

Kosher salt or coarse sea salt

1 large cannabis fan leaf, finely chopped

350ml/12fl oz/1½ cups soda water

Canola oil for frying

Fatima Ali runs Van Pakistan, a killer food truck that feeds Pakistani-inspired dishes, such as buttermilk fried chicken biryani, to hungry crowds at Brooklyn's Smorgasburg. When she came through the *Bong Appétit* kitchen, she blew everyone away with these gorgeous beetroot fritters, which will completely change your perspective on the generally yawn-worthy combo of beetroot and goat's cheese.

To make the goat's cheese sauce: In a small bowl, combine the goat's cheese, yogurt, infused olive oil and orange juice and mix well. Season with salt and pepper, cover and refrigerate until ready to use.

To make the pakoras: With a mortar and pestle, grind together the coriander seeds, cumin, chilli powder and kief until fine. Transfer to a large bowl. Add the beetroots, gram flour, 1 tablespoon salt, cannabis leaf and soda water and stir to form a loose batter. As the batter sits, the beetroots will release liquid, so add more gram flour as needed to maintain a good consistency.

Pour the canola oil to a depth of 8cm/3 inches into a large, wide, heavy saucepan and heat to 190°C/375°F on a deep-frying thermometer. Line a large baking tray with paper towels. Heat the oven to 80°C fan/100°C/200°F/gas ¼.

Working in batches to avoid crowding, drop heaped teaspoons of the batter into the hot oil and fry, turning the fritters as needed to cook and colour evenly, until lightly golden and crispy, about 4 minutes. Using a slotted spoon, transfer the pakoras to the prepared baking tray and keep warm in the oven. Repeat until all of the batter has been fried.

Season the pakoras with salt, then transfer to a serving plate and serve hot with the goat's cheese sauce.

Pro Tip: When deep-frying something that contains raw kief, the heat of the fryer can activate more of the THCA, converting it to THC. You're frying these fritters for only 4 minutes, so it's unlikely that much more decarboxylation will occur.

THC
3.5mg per potato skin;
28.6mg total recipe

Sweet Potato Skins with Pancetta and Chipotle Crema

MELISSA D'ELIA

Makes 8 potato skins

For the Weed-Infused Pancetta Fat

450g/1lb pancetta, in a single piece, cut into 5-mm/¼-inch cubes

1 gram cannabis trim, ground and decarboxylated (see page 54)

240g/8½oz/½ cup crème fraîche

2 tablespoons finely chopped fresh basil

2 tablespoons finely chopped fresh coriander

2 tablespoons finely chopped fresh mint

1 tablespoon finely chopped chipotle chilli in adobo sauce

2 spring onions, white and tender green parts, thinly sliced

4 sweet potatoes, scrubbed

225g/8oz/2 cups grated Gruyère, raclette or smoked Gouda cheese

Melissa D'Elia is a private chef with years of cannabis cooking experience (it's a hard job, but someone has to do it). One of the big takeaways she's gleaned over time is that if you're making something people are going to want to eat a lot of, you need to keep the dose low so folks don't accidentally end up too blazed to function. These potato skins fit the bill: they're ultra-low dose but ridiculously addictive. If this all feels like a lot to do at once (infusing the fat takes about 3 hours), you can infuse the pancetta fat and bake the potatoes ahead of time. Use any leftover infused pancetta fat for frying eggs on chill weekend mornings.

To make the weed-infused pancetta fat: Line a plate with paper towels.

In a large frying pan over a medium heat, cook the pancetta, stirring occasionally, until crispy and the fat has rendered, about 6 minutes. Using a slotted spoon, transfer the pancetta to the prepared plate and set aside. Pour the remaining fat into a 350-ml/12-fl oz canning jar, stir in the trim and seal tightly.

Stand the jar upright in a stockpot and add water until it is level with the top of the jar. Place the stockpot, uncovered, over a high heat and bring to a low boil. Let it boil for 2 hours, checking the water every now and again and adding more as needed to maintain the original level. After the first hour, 'burp' the jar by unsealing the lid to release any pressure build-up and then recap it.

After 2 hours, lay a tea towel on a heatproof work surface. Using an oven glove, remove the jar from the water, set it on the towel and leave to cool until it can be handled. Then, while the fat is still liquid,

continued

line a strainer with muslin and strain the fat into a measuring jug, squeezing any solids at the very end to extract all of the fat. Compost or discard the plant matter. Set the fat aside.

In the bowl of a food processor, combine the crème fraîche, 1 tablespoon each of the basil, coriander and mint, the chilli and 2 tablespoons of the spring onions. With the motor running, drizzle in 2 tablespoons of the infused pancetta fat, processing until well mixed. Transfer the crema to an airtight container and refrigerate until ready to use.

Heat the oven to 210°C fan/230°C/450°F/gas 8.

Wrap the sweet potatoes individually in aluminium foil and place on a baking tray. Bake for about 1 hour, until tender when pierced with a fork. Remove from the oven and leave to cool slightly. Leave the oven on.

Halve the warm sweet potatoes lengthways. Scoop out the flesh from each half, leaving walls about 1cm/½ inch thick (save the removed flesh for another use). Place the potatoes, skin-side down, on the baking tray and rub each one with 1 teaspoon of the infused pancetta fat, then sprinkle with the cheese and the cooked pancetta, dividing it evenly.

Bake the skins for about 20 minutes, until golden and crispy. Transfer to a serving platter and top each skin with 2 tablespoons of the crema. Sprinkle with the remaining 1 tablespoon each of basil, coriander and mint and the remaining spring onions, dividing them evenly. Serve immediately.

THC
0.9mg per spring roll;
22.5mg total recipe

Fried Spring Rolls

CHRISTINE HÀ

Makes 25 spring rolls

These Vietnamese-style spring rolls pack a riot of flavours into tight little packages. Writer and television host Christine Hà, who goes by 'The Blind Cook', has an incredible palate, which she puts to tremendous use building layers of flavour into everything she makes. On the show, Hà crumbled Diablo OG flower directly into the filling for these rolls, but we're going with raw kief here for a more controlled dose. Raw kief isn't nearly as potent as decarboxylated kief, so there's a lot of acidic THCA remaining in this ingredient. The quick but intense heat of the deep fryer may activate more THC, making the potency of these rolls variable.

Although you will be able to find some of the Asian-specific ingredients at any well-stocked supermarket, it is probably best to stop by your local Asian grocery store and pick up wood ear mushrooms, bean thread noodles, fish sauce and rice paper wrappers all at once.

To make the spring rolls: Bring a small pan of water to the boil over a high heat. Remove from the heat, add the mushrooms and leave to sit for 10 minutes; then drain, discarding the water.

In the bowl of a food processor, combine the mushrooms, noodles, carrot and onion and pulse until finely chopped. Transfer to a medium bowl.

Add the crab, garlic and shallot to the food processor and pulse until smooth. Transfer the crab mixture to the bowl with the mushroom mixture, then add the turkey, fish sauce, kief and egg and stir to mix well. Cover the filling and refrigerate for 1 hour.

Have ready a wide shallow bowl or pie plate of room-temperature water and a large platter or tray.

Submerge a rice paper wrapper in the water just until softened and pliable – about 20 seconds – then transfer it to a work surface. (Do not leave it in the water too long or it will soften too much and tear.) Place 2 tablespoons of the filling near the closest edge of the

continued

For the Spring Rolls

30g/1oz dried wood ear mushrooms

50g/2oz bean thread (glass) noodles, hydrated according to the instructions on the packet

½ carrot, peeled and coarsely chopped

¼ onion, coarsely chopped

50g/2oz white crabmeat, picked over for shell and cartilage fragments

1 garlic clove, thinly sliced

½ shallot, thinly sliced

115g/4oz minced turkey

1½ tablespoons fish sauce

0.5 gram raw kief

1 egg, lightly beaten

25 x 22cm/8½-inch round rice paper wrappers

For the Dipping Sauce

1 garlic clove, grated

1 fresh red chilli, deseeded (if desired) and finely chopped

Juice of 1 lime

125ml/4fl oz/½ cup water

60ml/2fl oz/¼ cup fish sauce

75g/2²⁄₃oz/6 tablespoons sugar

Canola oil for frying

Lettuce leaves for serving

Fried Spring Rolls, *continued*

wrapper. Roll the wrapper edge closest to you up and over the filling. Fold in the left and right sides of the wrapper, continue rolling away from you, tucking tightly as you go, until you reach the top edge, then press to seal the seam securely. Repeat with the remaining rice paper wrappers and filling, setting the rolls aside, seam-side down, on the platter as they are ready.

To make the dipping sauce: In a small canning jar or other jar with a tight-fitting lid, combine the garlic, chilli and lime juice. In a small bowl, whisk together the water, fish sauce and sugar until the sugar has dissolved. Add the fish sauce mixture to the jar, cover tightly and shake to combine thoroughly. Use right away, or store in the fridge for up to 2 weeks.

Pour the canola oil to a depth of 5cm/2 inches into a large, wide, heavy saucepan and heat to 180°C/350°F on a deep-frying thermometer. Set a large wire rack on a baking tray. Heat the oven to 80°C fan/100°C/200°F/gas ¼.

Vanessa Says: Crumbling Diablo OG adds a textural element to the dish as well as spicy flavours. Crumble some into your spring roll filling for an extra kick.

Working in batches to avoid crowding, add the rolls to the hot oil and fry, turning the rolls as needed to cook and colour evenly, until golden and crispy, about 8 minutes. Using tongs, transfer the rolls to the wire rack and keep warm in the oven.

Serve the rolls warm with lettuce leaves and the dipping sauce. Invite everyone to wrap a warm roll in a lettuce leaf before dipping.

THC

0.5mg per wonton;
11.3mg total recipe

With 60ml/2fl oz/¼ cup dipping
sauce: 4.7mg; 18.9mg total recipe

Pork Wontons

Nom Wah Tea Parlor

Makes 20 wontons and 240ml/8fl oz/1 cup sauce

For the Dipping Sauce

40g/1½oz/½ cup chilli flakes

1½ teaspoons kosher salt or
coarse sea salt

½ teaspoon sugar

3 garlic cloves, grated

210ml/7½fl oz/scant 1 cup
canola oil

1 tablespoon flower-infused
canola oil (see page 64)

For the Wontons

225g/8oz minced pork

20g/¾oz/½ cup finely chopped
fresh garlic chives

2 tablespoons black vinegar

2 tablespoons soy sauce

1 tablespoon peeled and grated
fresh ginger

3 garlic cloves, grated

0.25 gram raw kief

20 x 9cm/3½-inch square
wonton wrappers

Nom Wah Tea Parlor, a much-loved dim sum spot, has been a fixture in New York's Chinatown since 1920. Although plenty has changed in the world since then, Nom Wah's dumpling game remains entirely on point. While weed-infused chilli-garlic dipping sauce isn't something you'll find on the menu, it's a killer addition to these spicy, savoury wontons. If you're feeling bold, you can shake a little raw kief into the minced pork filling to make these dumplings a little more potent, or you can dose just the dipping sauce to keep things chill. You can usually find wonton wrappers in a well-stocked supermarket, but may need to visit an Asian market for the black vinegar (rice-based and inky black) and garlic chives (long, green and flat, with a faint garlic aroma).

To make the dipping sauce: In a small heatproof bowl, combine the chilli flakes, salt, sugar and garlic. In a small saucepan over a medium heat, combine both oils and warm to 120°C/240°F on a deep-frying or laser thermometer. Pour the hot oil into the bowl and whisk to mix well. Leave to cool for 1 hour, then use right away, or cover and refrigerate for up to 1 month.

To make the wontons: In a large bowl, combine the pork, chives, vinegar, soy sauce, ginger, garlic and kief and mix well.

Line a baking tray with baking parchment and have a small bowl of water nearby.

Line up about ten of the wonton wrappers on your work surface. Place about 2 teaspoons of the pork mixture in the centre of a wrapper and, using a fingertip dipped in the water, lightly dampen the outside edge of the wrapper. Fold the wrapper in half to form a triangle, taking care to press out any air pockets and pressing the edges to seal well. Now fold the two bottom corners of the triangle together, overlapping them slightly, and seal with a dab of water. Place the finished wonton on the prepared baking tray. Repeat with the remaining wrappers and filling. (If you like, you can freeze the wontons at this point. Slip the baking tray in the freezer, and when the wontons are frozen solid, transfer them to a ziplock freezer bag and freeze for up to 2 months.

They can be cooked directly from the freezer, adding 1 minute to the cooking time below.)

Bring a saucepan of water to the boil. Add the wontons and cook for about 2½ minutes. They are ready when they float to the surface. (If you want to make sure the filling is cooked through, scoop out a dumpling and check.) Using a wire strainer, lift them from the pan, shaking off any excess water, and transfer them to a platter. Serve warm with the dipping sauce.

THC
32.8mg per serving;
130.8mg total recipe

With Pot Pepperoni:
35mg per serving;
139.6mg total recipe

2 tablespoons flower-infused butter (see page 68)

1 tablespoon unsalted butter

1 tablespoon olive oil

2 garlic cloves, minced

1 onion, thinly sliced

2 x 400g/14oz cans whole peeled tomatoes, crushed by hand

Kosher salt (or coarse sea salt) and freshly ground black pepper

1 large loaf French bread, halved horizontally

450g/1lb mozzarella cheese, grated

225g/8oz/1 cup Homemade Ricotta Cheese (see page 233)

120g/4¼oz/1 cup thinly sliced Pot Pepperoni (see page 239; optional)

Fresh basil or cannabis fan leaves, thinly sliced, to garnish

Chilli flakes or grated Parmesan cheese, to garnish

French Bread Pizza

MUNCHIES Test Kitchen
Serves 4

This is what after-school snacks always hoped to grow up to be. If you're going for total DIY cred, make the ricotta cheese *and* pepperoni; if you're just trying to get high, the chunk of cannabis butter in the tomato sauce will take care of that nicely. (And no, you don't have to use either; or French bread, for that matter. This also makes a killer pizza bagel, pizza ciabatta, or pizza whatever-you-have-in-the-house.)

In a saucepan over a medium-high heat, warm both butters with the olive oil. Add the garlic and onion and cook, stirring occasionally, until soft, about 5 minutes. Add the tomatoes and cook, stirring occasionally, until the sauce is thick, about 15 to 20 minutes. Season with salt and pepper.

Remove from the heat and leave to cool slightly. Transfer to a blender and process until smooth.

Heat the grill.

Place the bread halves, cut-side up, on a baking tray. Spread about 225g/8oz/1 cup sauce on each half and top with mozzarella, ricotta and pepperoni (if using), dividing them evenly. Slide the baking tray under the grill and cook until the cheese is melted and golden and the pepperoni is crispy, about 4 minutes.

Remove from the oven, leave to cool slightly and then garnish with basil and chilli flakes. Cut each bread half in half again and serve.

THC

2.6mg per serving;
10.4mg total recipe

With kief: 8.6mg per serving;
44.5mg total recipe

Blackened Prawn Cocktail

COURTNEY MCBROOM

**Serves 4 (3 prawns per serving) and makes 125ml/4fl oz/
½ cup cocktail sauce (2 tablespoons per serving)**

For the Cocktail Sauce

60g/2¼oz/¼ cup ketchup

**2 tablespoons freshly squeezed
lemon juice**

**2 teaspoons grated fresh
horseradish**

**1 teaspoon Worcestershire
sauce**

**1 tablespoon flower-infused
olive oil (see page 64)**

For the Prawns

**2 teaspoons freshly ground
black pepper**

**2 teaspoons freshly ground
white pepper**

2 teaspoons cayenne pepper

2 teaspoons onion powder

2 teaspoons garlic powder

**2 teaspoons kosher salt or
coarse sea salt**

1 gram raw kief (optional)

**12 large prawns, peeled
and deveined**

2 tablespoons olive oil

Vanessa Says: When choosing
a variety of kief, opt for a bright
citrus aroma. Sour Diesel or a
Super Lemon Haze will work
well with the cocktail sauce.

Courtney McBroom is a proud Texas native who you absolutely cannot
expect to serve you a boring-ass poached prawn cocktail. Her version
blackens the prawns with a spice blend containing three types of
pepper, garlic powder and onion powder, plus a gram of kief that keeps
everybody happy.

Serve them up as old-school as your heart desires! Put the cocktail
sauce in the bottom of a martini glass and fan the prawns out on the
rim, with a lemon wedge in the mix for good measure. And, for
the love of God, if you happen to have decorative pot leaves on hand,
use as many as humanly possible (for flair).

To make the cocktail sauce: In a bowl, combine the ketchup, lemon
juice, horseradish, Worcestershire sauce and infused olive oil and stir
to mix well. Cover and refrigerate until ready to use.

To cook the prawns: In a small bowl, combine the black, white and
cayenne peppers, the onion and garlic powders and the salt and kief
(if using) and mix well.

Rinse the prawns and pat dry with paper towels. One at a time,
dredge each prawn in the spice mixture, coating evenly. Be generous,
as the more coverage you get, the more flavour you get!

In a large cast-iron or other heavy frying pan over a medium heat,
warm the olive oil until hot and shimmering. Add the prawns in a
single layer and cook them, without disturbing, until the underside
is nicely darkened, about 1½ to 2 minutes. Flip the prawns and cook
on the other side for 1½ to 2 minutes longer. The prawns should be
opaque throughout. They may burn a bit, and that's okay. You want
blackened prawns, not nicely browned prawns.

Transfer the prawns to a plate and serve immediately with the cocktail
sauce for dipping. Or, if you prefer to serve them in the classic prawn-
cocktail style, let them cool, then chill, uncovered, in the fridge for at
least 30 minutes or up to 1 hour before serving.

THC
11.7mg per serving;
93.6mg total recipe

Coconut Crab Gratin

MUNCHIES Test Kitchen
Serves 8

1 cup weed-infused coconut milk (see page 71)

2 teaspoons cornflour

450g/1lb jumbo lump white crabmeat, picked over for shell and cartilage fragments

2 tablespoons minced red onion

1 tablespoon finely chopped fresh coriander

½ teaspoon coconut sugar or granulated sugar

Grated zest and juice of 1 lime, plus lime wedges for serving

Kosher salt (or coarse sea salt) and freshly ground black pepper

Toast triangles for serving

Coriander and lime lighten up this delicate, sweet crab starter that's bound with infused coconut milk. If you have your pick of strains for infusing the coconut milk, select something on the citrusy side, like Super Lemon Haze or Tangie. Serving this gratin in natural crab shells is optional but baller. If crab shells are hard to come by, a small baking dish works fine, too.

Heat the grill.

In a small saucepan, whisk together the coconut milk and cornflour, then place over a medium heat and cook, stirring, until the mixture thickens, about 1 to 2 minutes. Remove from the heat and leave to cool slightly.

Add the crab, onion, coriander, sugar, lime zest and lime juice to the coconut milk and stir to mix well, then season with salt and pepper. Divide the crab mixture evenly among the crab shells and arrange the shells on a baking tray, or spoon the crab mixture into a small grill-proof baking dish.

Grill until the mixture is golden and bubbling, about 3 to 4 minutes. Serve hot with toast triangles and lime wedges.

Salads & Vegetables

THC
1.7mg per serving;
6.9mg total recipe

Cucumber and Citrus Salad

SARAH HYMANSON AND SARA KRAMER/KISMET

Serves 4

For the Za'atar

3 tablespoons hemp seeds, lightly ground

3 tablespoons sesame seeds, toasted and lightly ground

2 tablespoons ground sumac

1 teaspoon flower-infused olive oil (see page 64)

8 baby cucumbers, halved lengthways, deseeded and sliced crossways on the diagonal

1 teaspoon flower-infused olive oil (see page 64)

Juice of 2 lemons

Kosher salt or coarse sea salt

2 mandarin oranges, peeled and segmented

2 blood oranges, peeled and segmented

1 drop Green Crack terpenes (optional)

When Sarah Hymanson and Sara Kramer, usually of Kismet in Los Angeles but also of more cool side projects than we can count, appeared on *Bong Appétit*, they were new to cooking with weed but already total champions with farm-fresh produce, leafy greens and fresh herbs. Their take on *za'atar* – a popular Middle Eastern seasoning mixture that typically includes thyme and/or oregano, sumac, sesame seeds and salt – skips the usual herbs in favour of hemp seeds, which won't contribute to a high but do carry plenty of protein. Look for sumac in spice shops or Middle Eastern groceries and hemp seeds in health food stores.

To make the za'atar: In a small bowl, stir together the hemp seeds, sesame seeds, sumac and infused olive oil. The consistency should be such that the mixture is easy to sprinkle. Transfer to an airtight container and store in the fridge for up to 3 weeks.

In a medium bowl, toss together the cucumbers, infused olive oil and lemon juice and season with salt. Add all of the citrus segments and the terpenes (if using) and toss well. Transfer to a serving bowl, sprinkle with za'atar and serve immediately.

Vanessa Says: To brighten this salad and add some leafy greens, chiffonade some fan leaves to sprinkle on top. Did you know they pack more nutrients than kale?

THC
5.2mg per serving;
20.8mg total recipe

With Homemade Ricotta
Cheese: 21.2mg per serving;
84.8mg total recipe

Summer Tomato and Stone Fruit Salad

SAM SMITH/TUSK

Serves 4

For the White Wine and
Herb Vinaigrette

2 garlic cloves, minced

**3 tablespoons white wine
vinegar**

1 pinch Maldon sea salt

**10g/¼oz/½ cup loosely packed
fresh mint leaves, coarsely
chopped**

**10g/¼oz/½ cup loosely packed
fresh flat-leaf parsley leaves,
coarsely chopped**

6 tablespoons olive oil

**2 tablespoons flower-infused
olive oil (see page 64)**

**1 teaspoon crushed
Aleppo pepper**

Kosher salt or coarse sea salt

**450g/1lb mixed heirloom
tomatoes, cut into wedges, and
cherry tomatoes, halved**

**450g/1lb nectarines or peaches,
halved, stoned and cut into
wedges**

**15g/½oz/½ cup loosely packed
fresh basil leaves**

1 small red onion, thinly sliced

**45g/1½oz/⅓ cup almonds,
toasted**

**225g/8oz/1 cup Homemade
Ricotta Cheese (see page 233)**

Olive oil for drizzling

**Crushed Aleppo pepper
for sprinkling**

At the vegetable-forward, Israeli-inspired Tusk restaurant in Portland, Oregon, chef Sam Smith makes food that he likes to call 'aggressively seasonal'. This salad embodies that ethos, to an extent. Yes, it's the perfect dish for the height of summer, but the infused ricotta mutes any aggression you might be harbouring. And if you're not feeling ambitious enough to make infused ricotta, buy some good ricotta (from the Italian deli, please, not from the supermarket, and nothing with added stabilisers) and swap the regular olive oil in the dressing with additional infused olive oil instead.

To make the white wine and herb vinaigrette: In a small bowl, combine the garlic, vinegar and Maldon salt and leave to macerate for 5 to 10 minutes. Toss the mint and parsley with the vinegar mixture, then whisk in both oils and the Aleppo pepper. Season with kosher salt and set aside.

In a large bowl, combine the tomatoes and nectarines and toss to mix. Drizzle with the vinaigrette, sprinkle with the basil, onion and almonds and toss to coat evenly. Taste and adjust the seasoning if needed.

Transfer the salad to a plate (any liquid left behind in the bowl is great sopped up with bread). Dot the top of the salad with heaped tablespoons of the ricotta. Drizzle with a little olive oil, sprinkle with Aleppo pepper and serve immediately.

THC
5.2mg per serving;
31.2mg total recipe

BLAT Salad

MUNCHIES TEST KITCHEN
Serves 6

1 large loaf ciabatta, torn into 2.5-cm/1-inch pieces

3 tablespoons olive oil

Kosher salt or coarse sea salt

450g/1lb bacon rashers

3 tablespoons flower-infused olive oil (see page 64)

3 tablespoons red wine vinegar

450g/1lb mixed heirloom tomatoes, thinly sliced, and cherry tomatoes, halved

2 heads cos lettuce, roughly chopped

2 avocados, halved, peeled, stoned and diced

Freshly ground black pepper

This is the salad you eat when you're like, 'Shit, I should really eat a salad', but you're not willing to go full kale. In other words, this is a salad, but you're still putting bacon, fried bread and weed in it. Everyone's happy.

Heat the oven to 170°C fan/190°C/375°F/gas 5.

On a large baking tray, drizzle the bread with the regular olive oil, season with salt and toss to coat evenly. Spread the bread in an even layer on the tray. Bake until golden and crispy, about 10 minutes. Leave to cool completely.

Meanwhile, line a plate with paper towels.

In a large frying pan over a medium-high heat, cook as many bacon rashers as will fit without crowding, flipping once, until crispy, about 6 minutes on each side. Transfer the bacon to the prepared plate to drain, leave to cool slightly, then tear into bite-sized pieces. Repeat until all the bacon is cooked.

In a large bowl, toss the bread pieces with the infused olive oil and vinegar. Add the bacon, tomatoes, lettuce and avocados and toss to combine. Season with salt and pepper and serve immediately.

Vanessa Says: If you like bacon as much as I do, infuse the rendered fat with a pinch or two of kief (decarbed for a higher potency) and then toss the bread in a mixture of infused olive oil and the rendered infused bacon fat, before toasting in the oven.

THC
12.5mg per serving;
50mg total recipe

Creamy Coriander Kale Salad with Coconut 'Bacon'

JASMINE SHIMODA

Serves 4

1 bunch curly (about 450g/1lb) green kale, stems and ribs removed and leaves thinly sliced

125ml/4fl oz/½ cup Creamy Coriander Vinaigrette (see opposite)

30g/1oz/¼ cup Coconut 'Bacon' (see opposite)

55g/2oz/1 cup sunflower sprouts

35g/1¼oz/¼ cup sunflower seeds, toasted

20 cherry tomatoes, halved

4 radishes (purple or watermelon, if you can get them), peeled and chopped into 5-mm/¼-inch cubes

4 spring onions, white and tender green parts, thinly sliced

3 baby cucumbers, cut into 5-mm/¼-inch pieces

1 large avocado, halved, stoned, peeled and cubed

Kosher salt (or coarse sea salt) and freshly ground black pepper

Weed people like to say that cannabis is the new kale. This salad makes it clear that they can share the title. Jasmine Shimoda, of L.A.'s seminal yogi-hangout The Springs, has made more than a few kale salads in her time, and it shows. This one takes everything good about every kale salad you've ever had and synthesises it into a combination of perfectly tender kale, creamy green goddess-esque dressing (with a wholesome dose of THC) and crunchy smoky coconut 'bacon', which might be the only time something that isn't bacon lived up to bacon's good name. Alas, if you don't have a stove-top smoker and a dehydrator, you'll have to skip this inspired addition, but don't worry, the salad won't suffer as a result. The vinaigrette recipe makes more than you need for this salad, but leftovers would be killer smeared on a steak sandwich or used as a dip for crudités if you're fancy.

Put the kale in a large bowl. Drizzle with the vinaigrette, then, using your hands, massage the vinaigrette into the kale for a minute or two, until the kale feels softer. (This step breaks down the tough fibres and releases the natural sweetness of kale.) Add the coconut 'bacon', sunflower sprouts, sunflower seeds, tomatoes, radishes, spring onions, cucumbers and avocado and toss to mix well. Season with salt and pepper and serve immediately.

THC
25mg per 60ml/2fl oz/¼ cup;
320mg total recipe

Creamy Coriander Vinaigrette
Makes 700ml/24fl oz/3 cups

150g/5½oz/1¼ cups raw cashews, soaked overnight in water to cover

200ml/7fl oz/scant 1 cup freshly squeezed lime juice

Leaves and tender stems from 1 bunch coriander, coarsely chopped

1 bunch spring onions, white and tender green parts, coarsely chopped

½ jalapeño chilli, deseeded

Kosher salt or coarse sea salt

1 cup flower-infused grapeseed oil (see page 64)

Freshly ground black pepper

Drain the cashews, transfer to a blender and add the lime juice, coriander, spring onions, jalapeño and 1 tablespoon salt. With the motor running, slowly drizzle in the infused grapeseed oil until emulsified. Season with pepper, then taste and adjust the seasoning with salt. Transfer to an airtight container and store in the fridge for up to 5 days.

Coconut 'Bacon'
Makes 115g/4oz/2 cups

115g/4oz/2 cups unsweetened large coconut flakes

1 tablespoon liquid smoke

½ teaspoon smoked paprika

¼ teaspoon kosher salt or coarse sea salt

¼ teaspoon freshly ground black pepper

Prepare a stove-top smoker according to the manufacturer's instructions. Add the coconut and smoke for 10 minutes. Then, transfer the coconut to a bowl, add the liquid smoke, paprika, salt and pepper, and toss to mix well. Spread the seasoned coconut on a dehydrator tray and dehydrate at 45°C/115°F overnight, until dry and crispy. Transfer to an airtight container and store at room temperature for up to 2 weeks.

THC

5.2mg per serving;
20.8mg total recipe

With whipped infused honey:
7.5mg per serving;
30mg total recipe

North African Broccoli Salad

JOHN CLARK AND BEVERLY KIM/PARACHUTE
Serves 4

For the Ras el Hanout Vinaigrette

2 tablespoons flower-infused olive oil (see page 64)

150ml/5fl oz/scant ⅔ cup olive oil

2 tablespoons white balsamic vinegar

1 tablespoon ras el hanout

2 small garlic cloves, minced

2 tablespoons freshly squeezed lemon juice

2 tablespoons whipped weed-infused honey (see page 74; optional)

1 large head broccoli, cut into very small florets

10g/¼oz/¼ cup finely chopped fresh coriander

10g/¼oz/¼ cup finely chopped fresh mint

35g/1¼oz/¼ cup pistachios, toasted and finely chopped

10 Medjool dates, stoned and finely chopped

2 small shallots, finely chopped

1 jalapeño chilli, deseeded (if desired) and finely chopped

Kosher salt (or coarse sea salt) and freshly ground black pepper

Vanessa Says: Any time a recipe calls for herbs, add a few chopped fan leaves. It's a great way to use the whole plant and add a fresh bite to your dish.

This dish from John Clark and Beverly Kim, the husband/wife team behind Chicago's Parachute restaurant, puts the broccoli in broccoli salad – along with dates, *ras el hanout* (a North African spice blend), ground pistachios, coriander and mint. It's a series of unexpected flavours that somehow ends up working perfectly together – and it's even better after a day in the fridge.

To make the ras el hanout vinaigrette: In a small saucepan over a high heat, combine both oils, the vinegar, ras el hanout and garlic and bring to the boil. Lower the heat to maintain a steady simmer and cook for 5 minutes. Remove from the heat and strain through a fine-mesh strainer into a small heatproof bowl, discarding the solids. Whisk in the lemon juice and honey (if using) and set aside.

In a large bowl, combine the broccoli, coriander, mint, pistachios, dates, shallots and jalapeño and toss to mix. Drizzle with the dressing, season with salt and pepper and toss to coat evenly. Serve immediately.

THC
5.2mg per serving;
41.6mg total recipe

Hasselback Potatoes

MUNCHIES Test Kitchen

Serves 8

900g/2lb medium floury potatoes, scrubbed

2 rosemary sprigs, broken into many smaller sprigs

60ml/2fl oz/¼ cup flower-infused olive oil (see page 64)

60ml/2fl oz/¼ cup olive oil

Kosher salt (or coarse sea salt) and freshly ground black pepper

These potatoes have the dubious honour of being nearly everyone's favourite carb Instagram post, but they're more than just a pretty face. Slicing potatoes thinly before baking means tons of extra surface area to get crispy-crunchy in the oven – and to absorb all that infused oil.

Heat the oven to 200°C fan/220°C/425°F/gas 7.

Using a sharp knife, cut crossways slits about 5mm/¼ inch apart and about three-quarters of the way through the potato (so the slices remain connected at the bottom) along the length of each potato. Place the potatoes on a baking tray and stuff the slits with the rosemary, dividing it evenly. Drizzle the potatoes evenly with both oils, making sure that the oils reach down into the slits, then season with salt and pepper.

Roast the potatoes until crispy, golden and cooked through, about 1 hour. Serve immediately.

THC
4.7mg per serving;
18.7mg total recipe

Roasted Vegetables with Whipped Weed-Infused Honey

MUNCHIES Test Kitchen

Serves 4

450g/1lb baby potatoes, halved

350g/12oz golden beetroots, peeled and cut into wedges

150g/5½oz baby heirloom carrots, trimmed

230g/8oz Brussels sprouts, trimmed and halved

1 small acorn squash, halved lengthways, deseeded and thinly sliced crossways

3 tablespoons olive oil

Rosemary and thyme leaves for sprinkling

Cannabis leaves for sprinkling (optional)

Kosher salt (or coarse sea salt) and freshly ground black pepper

60ml/2fl oz/¼ cup whipped weed-infused honey (see page 74)

Infused honey fixes a multitude of sins – and plenty of things that aren't sins at all. Here, it works its magic on roasted vegetables, which are a classic for a reason. But they may as well be a classic for a reason that also gets you high.

Heat the oven to 200°C fan/220°C/425°F/gas 7.

On a baking tray, toss together the potatoes, beetroots, carrots, Brussels sprouts and squash. Drizzle with the olive oil, sprinkle with the rosemary, thyme and cannabis (if using), season with salt and pepper and toss again to coat evenly. Spread the vegetables in a single layer.

Roast the vegetables until golden, crispy and tender, about 30 minutes. Leave to cool slightly, transfer to a serving dish, drizzle with the infused honey and toss gently. Serve immediately.

THC
9.5mg per 115g/4oz/½ cup aioli;
37.8mg total recipe

Fried Mixed Mushrooms

ILIANA REGAN/ELIZABETH

Makes 4 servings and 450g/1lb/2 cups aioli

For the Aioli

2 heads garlic

2 tablespoons freshly squeezed lemon juice

2 teaspoons kosher salt or coarse sea salt

4 egg yolks

1 tablespoon water

2 tablespoons flower-infused canola oil (see page 64)

150ml/5fl oz/scant ⅔ cup canola oil

For the Mushrooms

85g/3oz/¾ cup acorn flour (use rye if you can't find acorn)

55g/2oz/½ cup rye flour

45g/1²⁄₃oz/⅓ cup plain flour

Kosher salt or coarse sea salt

1 teaspoon freshly ground black pepper

4 large eggs

75g/2½oz/1½ cups panko (Japanese bread crumbs)

450g/1lb mixed mushrooms (such as shiitake, chanterelles and button), stemmed if necessary and halved or broken into 5-mm/2-inch pieces

2 tablespoons canola oil, plus more as needed

4 tablespoons unsalted butter, plus more as needed

Maldon sea salt for finishing

Yes, we know. Acorn flour is a big ask of anyone. You do have a few options, however. You can either go full prepper and process and mill acorns that you hunt and gather yourself; you can score some acorn flour off the internet; or, tbh, you can just use all rye flour. That said, taking the trouble to source acorn flour is totally worth it, as this dish, from consummate cool-person Iliana Regan of Chicago's Elizabeth, radiates the kind of earthy vibes that will make you want to eat it in the middle of a mossy forest.

To make the aioli: Heat the oven to 180°C fan/200°C/400°F/gas 6.

Peel away the loose, papery outer skins from the garlic, leaving the heads intact. Wrap the garlic in aluminium foil and roast until a centre clove is completely soft when pierced with a knife, about 40 minutes. Remove from the oven, unwrap, leave to cool and then separate the cloves.

Squeeze the base of each clove to release the garlic from its skin, dropping the garlic into a blender. Add the lemon juice, salt, egg yolks and water and process for a few seconds until blended. With the motor running, very slowly drizzle in the infused canola oil. Once the mixture begins to thicken, add the regular canola oil in a thin, slow stream until all of the oil is incorporated and the aioli is smooth and thick. Transfer to an airtight container and store in the fridge for up to 2 weeks.

To make the mushrooms: In a medium bowl, whisk together all three flours, 1 tablespoon kosher salt and the pepper. In a second medium bowl, whisk the eggs until blended. Put the panko in a third bowl.

continued

Fried Mixed Mushrooms, *continued*

Working in small batches, dust the mushrooms in the flour mixture, shaking off the excess, then dip them into the eggs, allowing the excess to drip off. Finally, dredge them in the panko, coating them evenly and shaking off the excess. Set aside on a large plate.

Line a second large plate with paper towels.

In a large cast-iron frying pan over a medium-high heat, warm the canola oil and butter. When the butter begins to bubble, add the mushrooms, working in batches to avoid crowding, and cook, flipping them once and sprinkling them with kosher salt, until browned all over, about 3 minutes total. Now, tilt the pan towards you, collect the buttery cooking fat in a spoon, and baste the mushrooms, coating their sides and crevices. Once the mushrooms are well browned, using a slotted spoon, transfer them to the prepared plate. Season the mushrooms with Maldon salt and serve warm with the aioli.

THC

2mg per sandwich;
16mg total recipe

With infused butter:
16.7mg per sandwich;
133.6mg total recipe

The Collard Green Melt

MASON HEREFORD/TURKEY AND THE WOLF
Makes 8 sandwiches

Okay, so this isn't a salad. And it's not really a vegetable side, either. But it's so fucking good that it belongs here anyway. Dreamed up by Mason Hereford, a veteran of fine-dining kitchens who pitched it all to open Turkey and the Wolf (a chill sandwich spot in New Orleans), this sandwich is basically a cross between a club sandwich and a Reuben, with the addition of a mountain of greens (braised with more green). Your only job is to fit its layers of collard greens, coleslaw, Russian dressing, melted cheese and rye bread into your mouth. You'll need to tap a Korean market (or shop online) for the red pepper powder, as no substitute will do.

Diluting 60g/2oz/¼ cup of infused butter into 450ml/16fl oz/ 2 cups of pot liquor results in a THC dose of approximately 2mg per 1 tablespoon of liquid. Since most of the liquid remains in the stockpot and not on a sandwich, the cannabis is being used to flavour the collard greens and most of the psychoactivity is left behind in the liquor. Reserve the leftover liquor to make a vegetable soup, or alternatively use the optional infused butter to toast the bread.

For the Collard Greens

4 tablespoons flower-infused butter (see page 68)

55g/2oz/¼ cup minced garlic

125ml/4fl oz/½ cup red wine vinegar

125ml/4fl oz/½ cup rice vinegar

100g/3½oz/½ cup sugar

1 tablespoon Creole seasoning (we recommend Zatarain's brand, but others will work)

1 tablespoon Korean red pepper powder (gochugaru)

1½ teaspoons kosher salt or coarse sea salt

1½ teaspoons freshly ground black pepper

125ml/4fl oz/½ cup water

900g/2lb collard (or spring) greens, stems removed and leaves chopped

To cook the collard greens: In a large, heavy stockpot over a medium heat, warm the infused butter. Add the garlic and cook, stirring occasionally, until fragrant and cooked through, about 2 minutes. Add both vinegars, the sugar, Creole seasoning, red pepper powder, salt, black pepper and water and stir well. Cook, stirring occasionally, to allow the flavours to meld and develop, about 10 minutes.

Add the greens to the stockpot by the handful, waiting for each addition to wilt before adding the next. When all of the greens are added, cook, uncovered, over a medium-low heat, stirring occasionally, until the greens are incredibly tender, 2 to 3 hours. Remove from the heat, let the greens cool in their pot liquor and then reserve until ready to prepare the sandwiches. (Store in a covered container in the fridge for up to 5 days.)

For the Coleslaw

240g/8½oz/4 cups firmly packed thinly sliced green cabbage

85g/3oz/⅔ cup mayonnaise (we recommend Duke's brand)

2 tablespoons thinly sliced white onion

1 tablespoon distilled white vinegar

Kosher salt (or coarse sea salt) and freshly ground black pepper

continued

The Collard Green Melt, *continued*

For the Russian Dressing

55g/2oz/¼ cup coarsely chopped hot pickled cherry peppers

55g/2oz/¼ cup mayonnaise (we recommend Duke's brand)

¾ teaspoon ketchup

½ teaspoon Korean red pepper powder (gochugaru)

¼ teaspoon hot sauce (we recommend Crystal brand)

⅛ teaspoon smoked paprika

Kosher salt (or coarse sea salt) and freshly ground black pepper

8 tablespoons unsalted butter or flower-infused butter (see page 68), at room temperature

24 thin slices rye bread (with caraway seeds, if possible)

16 thick slices Emmental cheese

To make the coleslaw: In a large bowl, combine the cabbage, mayonnaise, onion and vinegar and season with salt and pepper. Using your hands, massage the cabbage to break it down in the mayonnaise until it is reduced to about one-quarter of its original volume. Taste and adjust the seasoning if needed, then cover and refrigerate until ready to use. (Store in a covered container in the fridge for up to 1 day.)

To make the Russian dressing: In a small bowl, stir together the cherry peppers, mayonnaise, ketchup, red pepper powder, hot sauce and paprika, mixing well. Season with salt and black pepper and set aside.

Using ½ tablespoon butter per slice, brush butter on both sides of three bread slices. Warm a non-stick griddle pan or a large non-stick sauté pan over a medium heat. Add the bread slices and toast on the first side until golden, about 1½ minutes. Flip the slices and top two of them with a cheese slice. Allow the cheese to melt fully, covering the slices with a pan lid to facilitate the melting process.

While the bread is toasting, in a sauté pan over a medium heat, warm a handful of the greens and about 4 tablespoons of pot liquor.

Place a handful of coleslaw on a cheese-up slice of rye bread. Place the second piece of cheese-up bread on top of the coleslaw. Spoon the warm greens on top of the second cheese-up slice, leaving some pot liquor behind (too much liquid will make the sandwich soggy). Dress the third slice of rye with a liberal slather of Russian dressing and place it, dressing-side down, on top of the greens. Cut the sandwich in half and serve immediately. Repeat to make the remaining sandwiches the same way.

Pasta & Grains

THC
11.5mg per serving;
46mg total recipe

Brown Butter Gnocchi

AURORA LEVERONI (AKA NONNA MARIJUANA)
Serves 4

For the Gnocchi

680g/1lb 8oz floury potatoes

1 tablespoon flower-infused olive oil (see page 64)

1 large egg, lightly beaten

½ teaspoon kosher salt or coarse sea salt

100g/3½oz/¾ cup plain flour, plus more for dusting

For the Brown Butter

170g/6oz/¾ cup unsalted butter

60g/2oz/¼ cup weed-infused brown butter (see page 70), at room temperature

Kosher salt (or coarse sea salt) and freshly ground black pepper

Grated Parmesan cheese for serving

Aurora Leveroni is the ninety-four-year-old mother of legendary cannabis crusader Valerie Leveroni Corral, co-founder of the Wo/Men's Alliance for Medical Marijuana (WAMM) in Santa Cruz, California. Known fondly as 'Nonna Marijuana', Aurora Leveroni focuses on creating infused food for the patients who need it most. These pillowy gnocchi are dosed in equal amounts with weed and love, Italian grandma-style. If you don't have a ricer (a metal basket with a perforated base through which the cooked potatoes are passed, yielding smooth, fluffy mashed potatoes), you can grate the potatoes on the large holes of a box grater, but you should probably get a ricer if you want the fluffiest-possible gnocchi.

There are a few ways to go about dosing this dish. Using the entire recipe of weed-infused brown butter adds a lot of flavour and more than 100 milligrams of THC. If each diner can handle a dose of 25 milligrams, that's probably the move. For a lower dose, do as this recipe directs and dilute 6g/2oz/¼ cup infused brown butter with 170g/6oz/¾ cup regular brown butter. Or you can rely solely on the weed-infused olive oil to get you high and use regular brown butter for dressing the gnocchi.

To make the gnocchi: In a medium saucepan over a high heat, combine the potatoes with water to cover generously and bring to the boil. Adjust the heat to maintain a gentle boil and cook until soft when pierced with a knife, about 30 to 35 minutes. Drain the potatoes, leave to cool just until they can be handled, then peel and discard the skins.

Pass the potatoes through a ricer held over a large bowl, taking care to remove any lumps. Add the infused olive oil, egg and salt and stir to combine. Then add the flour, a few spoonfuls at a time, mixing it in with your hands until all of the flour has been added and is evenly moistened and the dough begins to clump together. Knead the dough

continued

in the bowl until it is smooth, soft and a little sticky. This should take no more than a minute or two.

Line a large baking tray with baking parchment and dust the paper with flour.

Divide the dough into four equal pieces. Transfer one piece to a lightly floured work surface and, using your palms, roll the dough into a long rope about 2cm/¾ inch in diameter. Using a sharp knife, cut the rope crossways into 2.5-cm/1-inch pieces. Make an indentation in the centre of each piece by pressing your thumb into it while rolling it over the back of a fork. Transfer the finished gnocchi, in a single layer and not touching, to the prepared baking tray and cover with a tea towel. Repeat with the remaining dough. (The gnocchi will keep, covered with the towel, in the fridge until ready to cook or up to 24 hours. Alternatively, you can freeze the gnocchi on the baking tray, then transfer them to ziplock plastic freezer bags and freeze for up to 3 months; add them to the boiling water directly from the freezer.)

To make the brown butter: In a large frying pan over a medium-high heat, melt the unsalted butter. Cook for about 4 minutes, until the butter turns a light brown and has a nutty smell. Remove from the heat and stir in the infused brown butter. Set aside and keep warm until you have your gnocchi cooked.

Bring a large pot of generously salted water to the boil. Add the gnocchi and cook until they float to the surface, about 3 to 4 minutes. Using a slotted spoon, transfer the gnocchi to the pan with the brown butter and toss to combine. Season with salt and pepper and serve with Parmesan on the side.

THC
5.5mg per serving;
33.4mg total recipe

Green Mac and Cheese

MUNCHIES Test Kitchen
Serves 6

280g/10oz baby spinach

20g/¾oz/1 cup firmly packed
fresh flat-leaf parsley leaves

45g/1½oz/1 cup firmly packed
fresh basil leaves

80g/2¾oz/1 cup grated
Parmesan cheese

1 garlic clove

800ml/28fl oz/3½ cups
whole milk

2 tablespoons flower-infused
butter (see page 68)

2 tablespoons unsalted butter

45g/1½oz/⅓ cup plain flour

300g/10½oz/3 cups grated
white Cheddar cheese

Kosher salt (or coarse sea salt)
and freshly ground black pepper

450g/1lb elbow macaroni

A healthy amount of baby spinach and a healthier amount of infused butter turn this incredibly cheesy comfort-food classic green.

In the bowl of a food processor, combine the spinach, parsley, basil, Parmesan and garlic and pulse until chunky. Add 125ml/4fl oz/ ½ cup of the milk and process until smooth. Set aside.

In a large (6-litre/10-pint) saucepan over a medium-high heat, melt both butters. Add the flour and cook, stirring constantly, until thick and smooth, about 2 minutes. Continuing to stir constantly, add the remaining milk and then cook, stirring occasionally, until thick and creamy, about 8 to 10 minutes. Add half of the Cheddar and stir until melted. Season with salt and pepper.

Meanwhile, bring a large pot of salted water to the boil. Add the macaroni and cook, stirring occasionally, until al dente, according to the instructions on the packet.

While the macaroni cooks, heat the grill.

When the pasta is ready, drain it and add to the cheese sauce along with the spinach mixture. Stir to coat the macaroni evenly. Spread the macaroni mixture in a grill-safe 23 by 33-cm/9 by 13-inch baking dish, then top evenly with the remaining Cheddar. Set the baking dish on a baking tray and place under the grill until the top is golden brown and the macaroni and cheese is bubbling, about 5 to 7 minutes. Leave to cool for 10 minutes before serving.

Peanut Butter Noodles

MUNCHIES Test Kitchen

Serves 6

450g/1lb spaghetti

2 red peppers, deseeded and thinly sliced lengthways

1 cucumber, halved lengthways, deseeded and thinly sliced crossways

55g/2oz/½ cup crushed roasted peanuts

3 spring onions, white and tender green parts, thinly sliced

150g/5½oz/⅔ cup Homemade Peanut Butter (see page 232)

80ml/2½fl oz/⅓ cup soy sauce

50g/1¾oz/¼ cup firmly packed light brown sugar

80ml/2½fl oz/⅓ cup water

Fresh coriander leaves, to garnish

These super-easy noodles are like a 1990s Chinese-takeaway throwback, in all the best ways. Infused peanut butter lives its best possible life in the sauce here, but if you don't have any on hand, regular peanut butter with a little infused oil stirred in works just as well.

Bring a large pot of generously salted water to the boil. Add the spaghetti and cook, stirring occasionally, until al dente, according to the instructions on the packet. Drain the pasta, rinse under cool running water, drain again and transfer to a large bowl. Add the red peppers, cucumber, peanuts and spring onions and toss to mix.

Meanwhile, in a small bowl, whisk together the peanut butter, soy sauce, brown sugar and water until evenly incorporated into a sauce.

Add the sauce to the pasta and toss to coat the noodles and vegetables evenly. Transfer to a serving bowl and garnish with coriander. Serve immediately.

THC

5.5mg per serving;
33.4mg total recipe

With infused cream:
16.5mg per serving;
100.3mg total recipe

Sausage Pappardelle Bolognese

MUNCHIES Test Kitchen
Serves 6

2 tablespoons olive oil

2 tablespoons flower-infused butter (see page 68)

6 garlic cloves, finely chopped

1 carrot, peeled and finely chopped

1 celery stick, finely chopped

1 small onion, finely chopped

450g/1lb weed-infused sweet Italian sausage (see page 241), casings removed

½ teaspoon chilli flakes

Kosher salt (or coarse sea salt) and freshly ground black pepper

2 tablespoons tomato paste

125ml/4fl oz/½ cup dry red wine

2 x 400g/14oz cans whole tomatoes in juice, crushed by hand

90ml/3fl oz/6 tablespoons double cream

2 tablespoons weed-infused cream (see page 72; optional)

450g/1lb dried pappardelle

Grated Parmesan cheese for serving

Vanessa Says: Always follow your nose when picking varieties. In a Bolognese, Girl Scout Cookies or a peppery Bubba Kush will add a nice flavour to the overall dish.

The infused sausage works magic in this Italian-American dinner-table staple, which comes together much more quickly than a classic Bolognese sauce. If you're not up to at-home charcuterie, use shop-bought Italian sausage instead and dose the final dish with a drizzle of infused olive oil (see page 64) or a dollop of infused ricotta (see page 233). A few slivered fan leaves add a decorative finish.

In a large saucepan over a medium-high heat, warm the olive oil and infused butter. Add the garlic, carrot, celery and onion and cook, stirring often, until golden, about 8 to 10 minutes. Add the sausage and chilli flakes, season with salt and pepper and cook, stirring and breaking up the meat with a wooden spoon, until the sausage is crumbly, has lost its raw red colour and has browned, about 8 minutes.

Add the tomato paste to the pan and cook, stirring, for about 2 minutes. Pour in the wine, stir well to dislodge any browned bits on the pan bottom and boil gently until reduced by half, about 3 minutes. Add the tomatoes and bring to the boil. Lower the heat to maintain a simmer and cook, stirring occasionally, until the sauce is thick, about 6 minutes longer. Stir in the double cream and infused cream (if using) and simmer for 3 minutes to blend the flavours, then keep warm.

Meanwhile, bring a large pan of generously salted water to the boil. Add the pappardelle and cook, stirring occasionally, until al dente, according to the instructions on the packet. Drain the pasta, toss with the sauce and serve immediately. Pass the Parmesan around at the table.

THC
6.2mg per serving;
50mg total recipe

With cannabis flower:
6.3mg per serving;
51.5mg total recipe

Spinach and Artichoke Dip Risotto

MUNCHIES TEST KITCHEN
Serves 8

1.4 litres/48fl oz/6 cups chicken stock

6 cannabis fan leaves (optional)

5 whole black peppercorns

1 rosemary sprig

1 thyme sprig

0.5 gram cannabis flower, freshly ground (optional)

3 tablespoons flower-infused butter (see page 68)

1 large onion, diced

380g/13½oz/2 cups Arborio rice

240ml/8fl oz/1 cup dry white wine

140g/5oz baby spinach

40g/1½oz/½ cup grated Parmesan cheese

225g/8oz/1 cup cream cheese, at room temperature, cut into chunks

2 x 400g/14oz cans quartered artichoke hearts, drained

Kosher salt (or coarse sea salt) and freshly ground black pepper

Here's your favourite dip turned into a risotto, because we're classy like that. If you want to take it to the next level, a little extra freshly ground cannabis flower infused into the stock wouldn't hurt. Using cannabis as a spice adds extra flavour to this dish and works with the spinach without any further potency. You don't have to dip tortilla chips into it to keep it true to its dip origins. But, then, you also don't *not* have to.

In a saucepan over a medium-low heat, warm the chicken stock to a simmer. While the stock is heating, put the cannabis leaves (if using), peppercorns, rosemary, thyme and, if you're feeling flush, cannabis flower on a piece of muslin, tie together the corners to make a sachet and add the sachet to the stock. Keep the stock warm over a very low heat.

In a large (6-litre/10-pint) saucepan over a medium-high heat, melt the infused butter. Add the onion and cook, stirring often, until golden, about 6 to 8 minutes. Add the rice and cook, stirring occasionally, until lightly toasted, about 4 minutes. Pour in the wine and cook, stirring constantly, until evaporated, about 2 minutes. Add 125ml/4fl oz/½ cup of the warm stock and cook, stirring, until it has been absorbed, about 2 minutes. Continue adding stock, 125ml/4fl oz/½ cup at a time, stirring and cooking until it is absorbed before adding more, until the rice is tender and creamy. The total cooking time will be about 22 minutes.

Stir half of the spinach into the pan, allow the leaves to wilt completely, and then stir in the remaining spinach. Add the Parmesan, cream cheese and artichoke hearts and cook, stirring, until the cheeses have melted and the artichoke hearts are heated through. Season with salt and pepper and serve immediately.

THC

5.5mg per serving;
33.4mg total recipe

With kief: 9.2mg per serving;
55.6mg total recipe

Chicken Rice (*Riz a Djaj*)

REBECCA MERHEJ/LOVE & SALT

Serves 6

2 whole skin-on chicken breasts

1 cinnamon stick

Kosher salt or coarse sea salt

450g/1lb lean minced lamb

2 tablespoons flower-infused
butter (see page 68)

½ teaspoon freshly ground
black pepper

½ teaspoon ground allspice

½ teaspoon ground cinnamon,
plus more for sprinkling

0.5 gram raw kief (optional)

360g/12¾oz/1½ cups long-
grain white rice, rinsed and
drained

1 tablespoon vegetable oil

40g/1½oz/½ cup flaked or
slivered almonds

65g/2¼oz/½ cup pine nuts

110g/3¾oz/½ cup natural
whole-milk yogurt

Rebecca Merhej from L.A.'s Love & Salt made us this wildly satisfying chicken-lamb-rice bowl – just exactly what you want to curl up with at the end of a long day. It's what Lebanese grandma comfort-food would look like if your Lebanese grandma had access to high-end green and a generous hand with the seasoning.

Put the chicken breasts in a medium saucepan, add water to cover by 2.5cm/1 inch, the cinnamon stick and 1 teaspoon salt and bring to the boil over a medium-high heat. Turn the heat down to a gentle simmer, cover and cook until the chicken is opaque throughout and tender, about 20 to 30 minutes. Remove from the heat and transfer the chicken to a shallow bowl. Strain the cooking liquid through a fine-mesh strainer and reserve.

When the chicken is cool enough to handle, remove and discard the skin and then shred the meat. Return the chicken to the bowl, add a splash of the reserved cooking liquid and set aside.

Place a dry large frying pan over a medium heat. Add the lamb and cook, stirring and breaking up the meat with a wooden spoon, until the lamb has lost its raw red colour and is browned, about 10 minutes. Stir in the infused butter, 1½ teaspoons salt, the pepper, allspice, ground cinnamon and kief (if using), mixing well. Cover and cook for 10 minutes, stirring often to prevent sticking.

Add the rice and 570ml/20fl oz/2½ cups of the reserved cooking liquid to the frying pan, stir well, cover and bring to the boil. Lower the heat to a steady simmer and cook, covered, until the liquid is absorbed and the rice is tender, about 20 minutes.

While the rice cooks, line a plate with a paper towel.

In a medium frying pan over a medium heat, warm the vegetable oil. Add the almonds and pine nuts and toast, tossing or stirring constantly to prevent burning, until golden, about 4 minutes. Using a slotted spoon, transfer the nuts to the prepared plate to drain.

In a small bowl, stir together the yogurt and a pinch of salt, cover and refrigerate until ready to use.

When the rice mixture is ready, fluff it with a fork, then fold in half of the toasted almonds and pine nuts. Scoop the rice onto a serving platter and top with the shredded chicken. Garnish with the remaining pine nuts and almonds, sprinkle with a little ground cinnamon and finish with dollops of the yogurt.

Pro Tip: The nutty, cinnamony flavours here work well with earthy raw kief and spicy weed strains like Mazar Kush, Hindu Kush, Kosher Kush, Hash Plant and Red Dragon. If you're interested in significantly increasing the THC dose, toast your kief in an oven at 100°C fan/120°C/240°F/gas ½ for 30 minutes to decarboxylate it and activate more THC (see page 54).

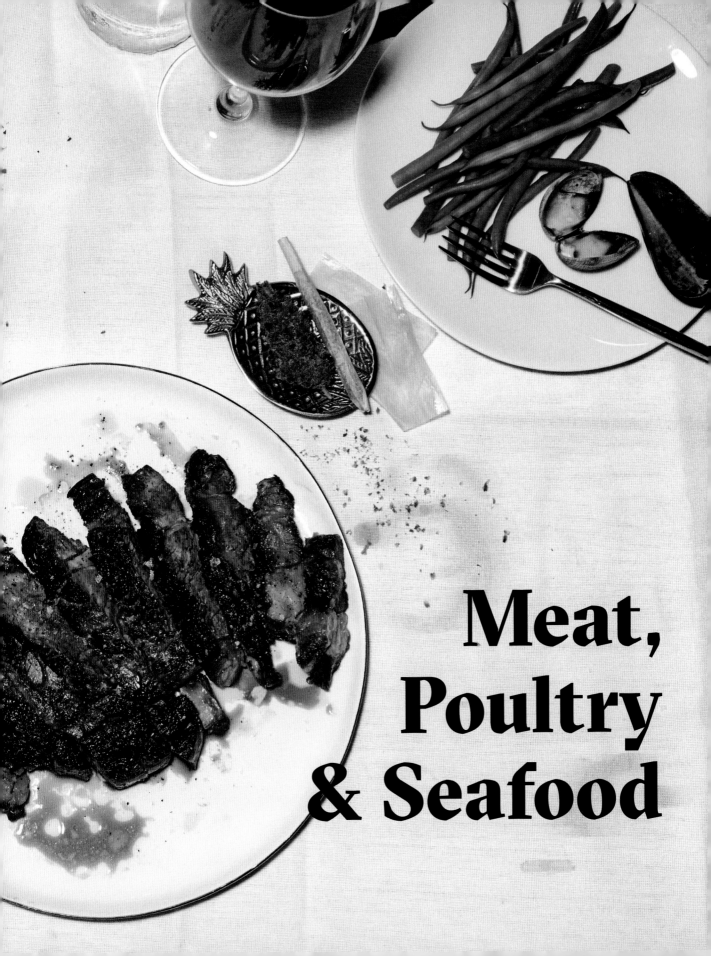

Meat, Poultry & Seafood

THC

5.2mg per serving;
10.4mg total recipe

With infused butter:
11.2mg per serving;
22.4mg total recipe

Rib-Eye with Weed Chimichurri

TIM MILOJEVICH

Serves 2

2 bone-in rib-eye steaks

Kosher salt (or coarse sea salt) and freshly ground black pepper

For the Chimichurri

Leaves from 1 bunch flat-leaf parsley, finely chopped

8 cannabis fan leaves, finely chopped (optional)

3 tablespoons red wine vinegar

1 tablespoon kosher salt or coarse sea salt

3 garlic cloves, minced

2 teaspoons dried oregano

1 teaspoon chilli flakes

1 tablespoon flower-infused olive oil (see page 64)

210ml/7½fl oz/scant 1 cup olive oil

2 tablespoons kief-infused butter (see page 68; optional)

Pot leaves don't get nearly enough credit. Sure, they're basically the universal symbol for weed, but there's also room for them in places that aren't necklaces, flags and cheesy tie-dyed T-shirts. Like this tangy chimichurri from private chef Tim Milojevich, where their vegetal notes shine alongside parsley and chilli. The leaves themselves aren't psychoactive but the olive oil they're mixed with is, and there's plenty of it.

Rub the steaks with a generous amount of salt and pepper. Leave to rest, uncovered, in the fridge for at least 10 hours or overnight. Remove the steaks from the fridge 2 hours before cooking to allow them to come to room temperature.

To make the chimichurri: In a medium bowl, combine the parsley, cannabis leaves (if using), vinegar, salt, garlic, oregano, chilli flakes and infused olive oil and stir to mix well. Transfer to an airtight container and store in the fridge for up to 2 days.

In a large cast-iron frying pan over a medium-high heat, warm the regular olive oil. Working with one rib-eye at a time, cook, flipping once, until well browned and cooked to your liking. The timing will depend on the thickness of the steak; a steak 2cm/¾ inch thick will take 8 to 10 minutes for medium-rare, or 57°C/135°F on an instant-read thermometer. Transfer the rib-eye to a chopping board and leave to rest for 10 minutes. Repeat with the remaining steak.

Cut the steaks against the grain into slices about 1cm/½ inch thick and transfer to individual plates. Serve topped with the infused butter, if desired, and accompanied with the chimichurri.

THC
4mg per serving;
16.7mg total recipe

Braised Short Ribs

THE PUBLICAN
Serves 4

For the Short Ribs

1.3kg/3lb beef short ribs

Green Hatch chilli powder for seasoning (use regular chilli powder if you can't get Green Hatch)

Kosher salt or coarse sea salt

2 tablespoons vegetable oil

2 carrots, peeled and diced

2 celery sticks, diced

1 onion, diced

2 thyme sprigs

1 bay leaf

450ml/16fl oz/2 cups red wine

1.8 litre/65fl oz/8 cups beef stock

For the Polenta

950ml/32fl oz/4 cups whole milk, plus more as needed

150g/5½oz/1 cup coarse-grind polenta

1 tablespoon flower-infused butter (see page 68)

7 tablespoons unsalted butter

Kosher salt or coarse sea salt

The Publican in Chicago is basically a shrine to high-quality, farmhouse-style meat-and-potatoes eating – to say nothing of the butcher shop next door. These braised, chilli-dusted short ribs are served on a bed of creamy weed polenta and finished with a briny, tangy samphire salsa verde. If you have it, a little raw kief or CBD-infused salt on the short ribs along with the salsa verde wouldn't necessarily be a bad thing – why should the polenta have all the fun?

To prepare the short ribs: Season the ribs all over with the chilli powder and salt. Place on a wire rack set on a baking tray and refrigerate, uncovered, for at least 8 hours or overnight.

Heat the oven to 150°C fan/170°C/325°F/gas 3.

In a large, heavy saucepan over a high heat, warm the vegetable oil. Working in batches, sear the ribs, turning them as needed to colour evenly, until golden brown all over, about 8 to 10 minutes. Transfer the ribs to a plate and set aside.

Add the carrots, celery, onion, thyme and bay leaf to the fat remaining in the pan and cook over a medium-high heat, stirring often, until the vegetables are slightly caramelised, about 7 minutes. Add the wine and bring to the boil, scraping up any browned bits on the bottom of the pan. Lower the heat to a steady simmer and leave to simmer until the wine is reduced by half, about 10 minutes. Return the ribs to the pan, pour in the beef stock, cover and cook until the meat is tender when pierced with a fork and almost falling off the bone, about 2½ to 3 hours.

To make the polenta: About 45 minutes before the ribs are ready, in a medium, heavy saucepan over a medium heat, bring the milk to a simmer. Gradually add the polenta to the simmering milk while stirring constantly to prevent lumps from forming. Turn the heat

continued

Braised Short Ribs, *continued*

For the Samphire Salsa

55g/2oz/1 cup marsh samphire

60ml/2fl oz/¼ cup champagne vinegar

60ml/2fl oz/¼ cup olive oil

2 tablespoons capers, rinsed and chopped

1 tablespoon honey

5 anchovies in olive oil, rinsed and chopped

4 small shallots, minced

½ jalapeño chilli, deseeded and minced

Kosher salt or coarse sea salt

Shaved ricotta salata for serving

Vanessa Says: Because the polenta calls for a lot of butter, adding more THC to this dish is easy. Just add infused butter instead of regular butter. A bold variety like Sour Diesel or OG Kush stands up to the richness of these ribs.

down to low and cook, stirring, until the polenta is smooth and creamy, about 25 to 30 minutes. Whisk in both butters and season with salt. Remove from the heat and cover to keep warm. You may need to add more milk before serving to keep it at the right consistency.

To make the samphire salsa: Fill a medium bowl with water and ice.

Bring a medium saucepan of generously salted water to a rolling boil over a high heat. Add the marsh samphire and cook for 1 minute, then drain and transfer the samphire to the iced water bath until cool. Drain the samphire and pat dry.

In a small bowl, whisk together the vinegar, olive oil, capers, honey, anchovies, shallots and jalapeño. Stir in the samphire and season with salt.

Divide the polenta evenly onto individual plates. Top with one or two short ribs, a spoonful or two of the salsa and some shavings of ricotta salata. Serve immediately.

THC
6.3mg per serving;
37.8mg total recipe

'Sugaree' Pork Ribs

Chris Lanter/Home Team BBQ
Serves 6

8 litres/14 pints water

280g/10oz/2 cups kosher salt or coarse sea salt

4 racks St Louis-cut pork spare ribs (about 900g/2lb each)

For the Alabama White Sauce

680g/1lb 8oz/3 cups mayonnaise (we recommend Duke's brand)

2 tablespoons flower-infused grapeseed oil (see page 64)

150ml/5fl oz/scant ⅔ cup grapeseed oil

2 tablespoons apple cider vinegar

2 teaspoons poppy seeds

2 teaspoons celery salt

Kosher salt (or coarse sea salt) and freshly ground black pepper

55g/2oz/½ cup mild chilli powder

3 tablespoons light brown sugar

1½ teaspoons kosher salt or coarse sea salt

1½ teaspoons freshly ground black pepper

These ribs, from Colorado chef Chris Lanter, might well be the most chill recipe in this book – they're literally named after a Grateful Dead song. Lanter takes St Louis-cut spare ribs (ribs with the tips cut off; if you can only get regular spare ribs, they'll be fine too), hits them with a simple rub of chilli powder and sugar and then roasts them until the meat falls off the bone. That's it. Seriously. While you're waiting for the ribs to finish, make the Alabama-style (aka mayo-based) barbecue sauce, which is where the magic (and weed) happens.

In a large, wide stockpot over a medium heat, bring the water to a simmer. Add the salt and stir until fully dissolved. Remove from the heat and leave the brine to cool completely. Add the ribs, immersing them fully in the brine, and let stand for 1 hour.

Remove the ribs from the brine and discard the brine. Lay the ribs in a single layer on a wire rack set on a baking tray and refrigerate, uncovered, for at least 8 hours or overnight.

To make the Alabama white sauce: In a medium bowl, combine the mayonnaise and both grapeseed oils and whisk until completely combined. Add the vinegar, poppy seeds and celery salt, season with kosher salt and pepper and stir until emulsified. Cover the bowl and refrigerate until ready to serve. Bring to room temperature.

Heat the oven to 90°C fan/110°C/225°F/gas ½.

In a large, wide bowl, stir together the chilli powder and brown sugar with the 1½ teaspoons salt and black pepper.

Add the rib racks to the bowl and rub them all over with the spice mixture, coating them evenly. Rinse the wire rack and baking tray and return the ribs to the wire rack in a single layer.

Roast the ribs for about 5 hours, until a knife slides easily into the thickest part of the meat. Let the ribs cool slightly, then cut them apart, pile them onto a large platter, and serve with the white sauce.

THC
5.2mg per serving;
10.4mg total recipe

Yogurt-Marinated Lamb

Erika Nakamura

Serves 2 (or 4 as a starter)

80ml/2½fl oz/⅓ cup olive oil

5 garlic cloves; 4 halved and
1 grated (optional)

4 thyme sprigs

2 rosemary sprigs

215g/7½oz/1 cup plain whole-
milk Greek yogurt

2 tablespoons red wine vinegar

Kosher salt (or coarse sea salt)
and freshly ground black pepper

1 rack of lamb (8 chops),
at room temperature

1 tablespoon flower-infused
olive oil (see page 64)

Lemon wedges for squeezing

Erika Nakamura is a butcher's butcher. She's spent a long stint at New York City's White Gold, along with partner Jocelyn Guest, and co-founded L.A.'s Lindy and Grundy – so it's no surprise that she'd come up with the goods here. A grilled rack of lamb is one of those impressive-af dinner-party foods where no one needs to know how difficult it actually wasn't. Pair this with the tomato and stone fruit salad on page 120 and with a pinier, skunkier strain of cannabis, like an old-school Afghani or Shiva Senti, to bring out the herb notes in the lamb. Either strain would work just as well in the olive oil as it would in a joint beforehand.

In a small saucepan over a medium-low heat, combine the olive oil, halved garlic, thyme and rosemary, bring to a gentle simmer and cook for about 15 minutes. Remove from the heat and leave to cool completely. Transfer to a large bowl and stir in the yogurt, vinegar and grated garlic (if using). Season the marinade with salt and pepper.

Add the lamb to the marinade and turn to coat evenly. Cover and refrigerate for at least 8 hours or up to 24 hours.

Prepare a charcoal or gas grill or barbecue for indirect-heat grilling.

Remove the lamb from the marinade, scraping off most of the marinade and being careful to remove any bits of herb, and bring to room temperature.

When the fire is ready, place the lamb rack, bone-side down, on the grill directly over the fire and cook until lightly browned, about 3 to 4 minutes. Flip the lamb, placing it meat-side down over indirect heat, and cook to your liking, about 10 minutes for medium-rare or 50–55°C/125–130°F on an instant-read thermometer.

Transfer the lamb to a chopping board and leave to rest for about 10 minutes, then carve between the bones into individual chops. Divide onto individual plates and drizzle with the infused olive oil and a squeeze of lemon juice. Serve immediately.

THC
5.7mg per serving;
22.8mg total recipe

Double-Lemon Roast Chicken

JOAN NATHAN
Serves 4

1.3–1.8kg/3–4lb whole chicken

2 tablespoons flower-infused olive oil (see page 64)

Kosher salt (or coarse sea salt) and freshly ground black pepper

1 to 2 tablespoons za'atar

1 teaspoon ground sumac

1 preserved lemon (see page 228), halved and one half diced

8 thyme sprigs

4 rosemary sprigs

2 sage sprigs

1 onion, cut into about 8 pieces

2 lemons, thinly sliced into rounds

1 celery stick, cut into 5-cm/ 2-inch pieces

1 carrot, peeled and cut into 5-cm/2-inch pieces

1 fennel bulb, trimmed and cut into 5-cm/2-inch pieces

185ml/6fl oz/¾ cup dry white wine

Joan Nathan is basically the grand dame of Jewish home cooking. Even though she had never even seen weed in her life before coming on *Bong Appétit*, she was completely down to experiment. The result? This ultra-lemony roast chicken that uses both fresh lemons and preserved lemons to maximum advantage. Use a citrusy strain of herb, like Lemon Skunk, to round out the experience.

Heat the oven to 170°C fan/190°C/375°F/gas 5.

Rub the chicken with the infused olive oil, then season with salt, pepper, as much of the za'atar as you like and the sumac.

Place the chicken, breast-side up, in a 23 by 33-cm/9 by 13-inch baking dish. Put the preserved lemon half and a sprig each of the thyme, rosemary and sage in the cavity. Scatter the onion pieces, lemon slices, diced preserved lemon, celery, carrot, fennel and remaining thyme, rosemary and sage around the chicken.
Pour in the wine.

Roast the chicken until golden brown and crispy and an instant-read thermometer inserted into the thickest part of the thigh away from bone registers 75°C/165°F, about 1¼ hours.

Remove the chicken from the oven, leave to rest for about 10 minutes and then cut into eight pieces. Arrange the pieces on a platter and spoon the vegetables, preserved lemon, lemon slices and pan juices over and around the chicken. Serve immediately.

THC
5.8mg per serving;
34.9mg total recipe

Korean Fried Chicken

DEUKI HONG/SUNDAY BIRD
Serves 2

For the Kimchi Ganja Salt

2 tablespoons onion powder

1 tablespoon garlic powder

1 tablespoon shrimp powder

1 teaspoon citric acid powder

1 teaspoon coconut sugar or granulated sugar

1 teaspoon ground ginger

1 gram cannabis flower, ground and decarboxylated (see page 54)

35g/1¼oz/¼ cup kosher salt

For the Marinade

60ml/2fl oz/¼ cup olive oil

60ml/2fl oz/¼ cup soy sauce

3 tablespoons kosher salt

12 garlic cloves

1 onion, quartered through the stem end

Grated zest and juice of 1 lemon

900g/2lb chicken wings

100g/3½oz/1 cup cornflour

Canola oil for frying

For the Batter

135g/4¾oz/1 cup plain flour

100g/3½oz/1 cup cornflour

1 teaspoon baking powder

240ml/8fl oz/1 cup soju or vodka

240ml/8fl oz/1 cup water

Deuki Hong, chef at Sunday Bird in San Francisco, said he had never cooked with weed before he came on *Bong Appétit*. But after tasting his infused food, we're not sure we believe him. Between the killer kimchi fried rice he made on the show and these crispy, spicy Korean-style fried chicken wings, he's clearly some kind of weed savant. The kimchi ganja salt that tops these wings is a versatile addition to other dishes, too. You might use it to perk up (or mellow out) scrambled eggs, or fold it into softened butter for topping a grilled steak.

This recipe has a lot of steps and calls for some ingredients you might need to seek out via speciality Asian stores or (gasp) the internet. Edible citric acid, a sour-tasting powder, is a good example of an ingredient you'll probably need to hunt down from online retailers. We promise the search is worth it.

To make the kimchi ganja salt: Using a mortar and pestle, combine the onion powder, garlic powder, shrimp powder, citric acid, sugar, ginger and cannabis flower and grind to a fine powder. Alternatively, combine the ingredients in a spice grinder and grind to a fine powder. Transfer the ground mixture to a small bowl, add the salt and stir to combine. Transfer to an airtight container and store in the fridge for up to 3 months.

To make the marinade: In a blender, combine the olive oil, soy sauce, salt, garlic, onion, lemon zest and lemon juice and process until smooth.

Poke holes all over the chicken wings with a fork. In a large bowl, toss the wings with the marinade until evenly coated. Cover and refrigerate for at least 2 hours or overnight.

Place a wire rack on a baking tray.

Remove the chicken wings from the marinade, allowing the excess to drip off, and place in a clean large bowl. Toss with the cornflour, coating evenly, then transfer to the wire rack and leave to sit at room temperature for 30 minutes (this allows the cornflour to hydrate and form a skin on the wings).

Vanessa Says: This is one of the rare occasions when you can grind decarboxylated flower with everything else in the salt blend, as it's getting paired with a fat that will help absorb it. Choose a spicy, earthy flower like Northern Lights or Kosher Kush; toasting brings out a nuttier flavour as well as activates the THC.

Pour the canola oil to a depth of 8cm/3 inches in a large, wide, heavy saucepan and heat to 180°C/350°F on a deep-frying thermometer. Line a plate with a double thickness of paper towel.

To make the batter: While the oil heats, in a medium bowl, combine the plain flour, cornflour, baking powder, soju and water and stir until the mixture has the consistency of watered-down glue.

Working in batches, dip the wings in the batter and let the excess drip off. Transfer the wings to the hot oil, a few at a time, and fry, turning as needed to colour evenly, until golden brown and an instant-read thermometer inserted into the thickest part of a wing away from bone registers 175°C/165°F, about 4½ minutes. Using a slotted spoon, transfer the wings to the prepared plate to drain. Then, transfer to a large platter and sprinkle each wing with an equal amount of the ganja salt. Serve hot.

THC

2.3mg per serving;
18.4mg total recipe

With kief: 7.8mg per serving;
62.9mg total recipe

Pakalolo Poke Bowl

Sheldon Simeon/Tin Roof

Serves 8

For the Poke

450g/1lb sashimi-grade tuna,
cut into 1cm/½-inch cubes

1 small sweet onion,
finely chopped

1 teaspoon sea salt

2cm/¾-inch piece fresh ginger,
peeled and grated

1 tablespoon flower-infused
sesame oil (see page 64)

1 tablespoon Sriracha

1 tablespoon sambal oelek

1 tablespoon oyster sauce

2 tablespoons soy sauce

65g/2¼oz/¼ cup masago (capelin
roe) or salmon roe

55g/2oz/¼ cup mayonnaise

For the Sweet Soy Sauce

60ml/2fl oz/¼ cup soy sauce

50gml/1¾oz/¼ cup sugar

1½ tablespoons mirin

1½ tablespoons sake

1 tablespoon dashi powder
(Japanese stock base)

125ml/4fl oz/½ cup water,
plus 1½ tablespoons

2 tablespoons cornflour

750g/1lb 10oz/6 cups cooked
long-grain white rice (about
300g/10oz/2½ cups uncooked)

1 spring onion, white and tender
green parts, thinly sliced

Furikake (dried Japanese
seasoning), rice crackers and/or
dried seaweed powder, to garnish

1 gram raw kief (optional)

Chef Sheldon Simeon of Maui's Tin Roof restaurant is a man who takes his poke seriously. When he came through our office to make a traditional poke for us, he casually pulled a bag of ground inamona nuts – nearly impossible to find outside of Hawaii, but classic for purists – out of his backpack, knowing that the poke wouldn't be the same without them. Think of weed as the inamona nuts of this less-traditional poke; it just adds that extra something.

To make the poke: In a large bowl, combine the tuna, onion, sea salt and ginger and fold together to mix evenly. Add the infused sesame oil, Sriracha, sambal oelek, oyster sauce, soy sauce, masago and mayonnaise and gently fold together until well mixed.

To make the sweet soy sauce: In a small saucepan over a medium-high heat, combine the soy sauce, sugar, mirin, sake, dashi powder and 125ml/4fl oz/½ cup water and bring to the boil, stirring occasionally. Lower the heat to a simmer and cook for 10 minutes to blend the flavours.

Meanwhile, in a small bowl, stir together the cornflour and remaining 1½ tablespoons water to make a slurry. While stirring constantly, slowly add the slurry to the soy sauce mixture, then continue stirring until the mixture thickens to a syrupy consistency. Remove from the heat and set aside to cool.

Divide the rice evenly into eight bowls. Scoop the poke over the rice, dividing it evenly, and drizzle each serving with about 1 tablespoon of the sweet soy sauce. Garnish the rice with the spring onion, furikake and rice crackers, then dust the bowls with the seaweed powder and the kief (if using). Serve immediately.

THC

8.4mg per serving;
33.4mg total recipe

Swordfish Teriyaki

Yoya Takahashi/Umi by Hamasaku
Serves 4

4 x 140g/5oz swordfish or
halibut fillets

Kosher salt (or coarse sea salt)
and freshly ground black pepper

2 tablespoons flower-infused
butter (see page 68)

350/12fl oz/1½ cups Homemade
Teriyaki Sauce (see below)

Toasted sesame seeds,
to garnish

Spring onions, white and tender
green parts, sliced, to garnish

Cooked short-grain white rice
for serving

So simple, so easy, so good. Frankly, we'd expect nothing less from
sushi master Yoya Takahashi of L.A.'s Hamasaku restaurant. Swordfish
is a meaty, almost steaky fish, so it does well with strong flavours like
this salty-sweet, pot butter-laced teriyaki glaze. Hit this with some
toasted sesame seeds and sliced spring onions, drop it on a bowl of
short-grain rice and enjoy your night.

Heat the oven to 180°C fan/200°C/400°F/gas 6.

Season the fish all over with salt and pepper.

In a large cast-iron or other heavy ovenproof frying pan over
a medium-high heat, melt the infused butter. When the foam
subsides, add the fish and cook until cooked halfway through, about
2½ minutes (timing will depend on the thickness of the fillets;
plan on 10 minutes total for fillets 2.5cm/1 inch thick). Flip the fish
and transfer the pan to the oven until the fish is cooked 80 per cent
through, about 5 minutes.

Return the pan to the stove top over a low heat, pour in the teriyaki
sauce, and cook, basting the fish occasionally with the sauce, until
the fish is cooked through, about 3 minutes longer. Transfer the fish
to a plate and keep warm. Continue reducing the sauce over a low
heat until thickened, about 10 minutes.

Pour the thickened sauce over the fish, garnish with sesame seeds
and spring onions and serve immediately with rice.

Homemade Teriyaki Sauce
Makes 800ml/28fl oz/3½ cups

240ml/8fl oz/1 cup mirin

240ml/8fl oz/1 cup sake

240ml/8fl oz/1 cup soy sauce

100g/3½oz/½ cup sugar

In a medium bowl, combine the mirin, sake, soy sauce and sugar
and whisk until fully incorporated. Transfer to an airtight container
and store in the fridge for up to 2 months.

THC
10.4mg per serving;
41.6mg total recipe

With rosin and cannabis flower:
38.6mg per serving;
154.2mg total recipe

Grilled Whole Sea Bream

DAVID WILCOX/JOURNEYMEN
Serves 4

125ml/4fl oz/½ cup flower-infused olive oil (see page 64)

1 gram rosin (see page 22; optional)

4 whole, head-on black sea bream or bass, cleaned

Kosher salt (or coarse sea salt) and freshly ground black pepper

4 grams cannabis flower, ground (optional)

85g/3½oz/3 cups mixed fresh herbs and greens (such as cannabis fan leaf, flat-leaf parsley, coriander and winter purslane or baby spinach)

2 lemons, thinly sliced, plus freshly squeezed lemon juice for dressing

Extra-virgin olive oil for dressing

Vanessa Says: Fish and cannabis' bright limonene notes are an ideal match, especially with the herbs in this dish. Use a citrus-scented rosin like Tangie or Lemon Haze on the inside of the cavity before stuffing with herbs.

Whole fish stuffed with herbs and grilled over an open fire is a pretty incredible summer dinner. Grilled whole fish stuffed with herbs *and* herb – now that's just next-level. When chef David Wilcox of L.A.'s Journeymen made this on the show, he brushed the fish inside and out with weed-infused olive oil, then stuffed it with extra rosin and buds. But Wilcox's speciality is local and foraged ingredients, so he's flexible, and his recipe is more of a guideline. Pretty much any combination of herbs, greens and lettuces will work just fine here, along with as much rosin and bud as you think your guests may want to handle.

Build a hot fire for direct-heat grilling in a charcoal grill or heat a gas grill to medium-high.

In a small saucepan over a low heat, warm the infused olive oil (just to the touch). Add the rosin (if using) and stir to dissolve.

Pat the fish dry inside and out. Score the skin in a few places on both sides of each fish, making the slashes perpendicular to the backbone and just deep enough to expose some flesh. Rub each fish, inside and out, with the warm oil, then season liberally inside and out with salt and pepper. Place 1 gram of the cannabis flower in the cavity of each fish, then take two-thirds of the mixed herbs and stuff an equal amount into each cavity so the cannabis does not fall out. Line each fish cavity with the lemon slices, overlapping them slightly.

When the fish are ready for grilling, check the heat of the grill; it is ready when you can hold your hand 13cm/5 inches above the heat for 4 to 6 seconds before having to pull it away. Place the fish on the grill rack and cook for 7 to 9 minutes, flipping them once halfway through the cooking time. The skin should be crisp and the flesh supple and opaque throughout.

Just before serving, in a medium bowl, toss the remaining mixed herbs and greens with a splash each of lemon juice and extra-virgin olive oil and season with salt. Transfer the fish to individual plates and serve with the dressed greens.

THC
8.4mg per serving;
50mg total recipe

Grilled Oysters

MUNCHIES Test Kitchen
Serves 6

2 tablespoons olive oil

1 bunch ramps or wild garlic, trimmed and thinly sliced

200g/7oz/¾ cup plus 2 tablespoons unsalted butter, at room temperature, plus more for the coals

3 tablespoons flower-infused butter (see page 68)

Grated zest and juice of 1 lemon

Kosher salt (or coarse sea salt) and freshly ground black pepper

36 oysters

There are basically two truths about oysters: They are a great way to start off a meal, and they are a total pain in the ass to shuck, especially for a crowd. Make someone else shuck the oysters while you set up the grill. You'll hear some complaining, but that will stop when the weed butter hits. If you can't find ramps locally or don't know where to forage for them in the wild, substitute the tops of spring onions and a garlic clove or two.

In a 25-cm/10-inch frying pan over a medium-high heat, warm the olive oil. Add the ramps and cook, stirring often, until soft, about 2 to 3 minutes. Transfer to a bowl, add both butters, the lemon zest and lemon juice and mix well. Season with salt and pepper and then set aside.

Using an oyster knife, shuck each oyster, lifting off and discarding the top shell and leaving the oyster in the bottom (more cup-shaped) shell. Slide the knife under the oyster to sever the muscle attaching it to the shell.

Light a fire for direct-heat grilling in a charcoal grill. Once hot, place a small dollop of unsalted butter directly on the coals and cover the grill until it starts to smoke.

Top each oyster with an equal amount of the butter mixture. Place the oysters on the grill rack and immediately cover the grill. Cook until the oysters are plump and their edges begin to curl slightly, about 2 to 3 minutes. Using tongs, carefully transfer the oysters to individual plates or a couple of large serving platters. Serve immediately.

THC
5.2mg per serving;
41.6mg total recipe

Fried Soft-Shell Crab with Shishito Pepper Mole

Daniela Soto-Innes/Cosme/Atla
Serves 8

For the Mole

60ml/2fl oz/¼ cup flower-infused olive oil (see page 64)

60ml/2fl oz/¼ cup olive oil

3 garlic cloves, sliced

200g/7oz shishito or padrón peppers, stemmed

8 serrano chillies, halved and deseeded

Leaves and tender stems from 1 bunch coriander

225g/8oz/1 cup small ice cubes

1 tablespoon kosher salt or coarse sea salt

3 tablespoons yuzu juice

3 tablespoons freshly squeezed lime juice

For the Tempura Batter

150g/5½oz/1½ cups cornflour (cornstarch)

150g/5½oz/1 cup fine cornmeal (polenta)

1 tablespoon bicarbonate of soda

1 teaspoon kosher salt or coarse sea salt

450ml/16fl oz/2 cups soda water, chilled

Soft-shell crabs done right don't actually need much in the way of accompaniments, but this recipe, from Daniela Soto-Innes of New York City's Mexican legend Cosme and all-day cafe Atla, blew our fucking minds. Perfectly crunchy, juicy fried soft-shell crabs might not *need* a just-spicy enough (and just-heady enough) shishito pepper mole and smoky roasted tomatoes, but you'll never want to eat them without either again. Plus, adding the infused oil to the mole makes portioning and dosing this dish easy. The combination of cornflour and cornmeal keeps the crabs crunchy; look for fine-grade cornmeal (polenta) in well-stocked supermarkets, natural food stores or online.

To make the mole: In a medium saucepan over a medium heat, warm both oils. When the combined oil is hot, add the garlic and cook, stirring, until translucent, about 1 minute. Add the shishitos and serranos and cook, stirring occasionally, until the shishitos burst, about 5 minutes. Transfer the contents of the pan to a blender. Add the coriander, ice cubes, salt, yuzu juice and lime juice and process until smooth. Pass through a fine-mesh strainer into a medium bowl and set aside at room temperature.

To make the tempura batter: In a medium bowl, stir together the cornflour, cornmeal, bicarbonate of soda and salt. Transfer to the freezer and chill for 20 minutes. Remove from the freezer and stir in the soda water; the batter should be relatively thick. Keep the batter refrigerated until ready to use.

continued

Fried Soft-Shell Crab with Shishito Pepper Mole, *continued*

150g/5½oz/1½ cups cornflour

Vegetable oil for frying

8 soft-shell crabs, cleaned (your fishmonger can do this for you)

For the Roasted Tomatoes

340g/12oz yellow cherry tomatoes

2 tablespoons olive oil

1 teaspoon kosher salt or coarse sea salt

8 limes, halved

40 fresh lemon balm leaves

Vanessa Says: When I see coriander, I think of the cannabis fan leaves. More tender, smaller leaves blitzed with the tender coriander leaves will add another depth to this mole. The shiso flavour of the leaves will play off the yuzu acid notes.

Line a baking tray with paper towels and set near the stove. Spread the second 150g/5½oz/1½ cups cornflour in a wide, shallow medium bowl.

Pour the vegetable oil to a depth of 5cm/2 inches in a heavy, medium stockpot and heat to 190°C/375°F on a deep-frying thermometer. Working with one crab at a time, dredge the crab in the cornflour, coating evenly on all sides and tapping off the excess. Using tongs, dip the crab into the batter, letting the excess drip off, then lower the crab gently into the hot oil. Fry until golden and crispy, turning it once at the halfway point, about 4 minutes total. Using the tongs, transfer the crab to the prepared baking tray to drain.

To make the roasted tomatoes: Heat the grill. Line a baking tray with baking parchment.

Pile the tomatoes on the prepared baking tray. Drizzle with the olive oil, sprinkle with the salt and toss to coat evenly. Spread the tomatoes in a single layer and grill just until they begin to burst, about 2 to 3 minutes.

Divide the mole evenly among individual plates, spreading it out, and top each plate with a few tomatoes and a crab. Squeeze a lime half over each crab and garnish with 5 lemon balm leaves. Alternatively, spread the mole on a large serving platter, top with the tomatoes and crabs, squeeze half of the lime halves over the top and garnish with the lemon balm leaves. Serve immediately, with the remaining lime halves on the side.

THC
3.3mg per serving;
20mg total recipe

Green Shellfish Curry

LOUIS TIKARAM/E.P & L.P.

Serves 6

950ml/32fl oz/4 cups chicken stock

240ml/8fl oz/1 cup coconut cream

10g/¼oz/¼ cup kaffir lime leaves

2 lemongrass stalks, grass tops removed and then bashed to release their flavour

55g/2oz/¼ cup Homemade Curry Paste (see opposite)

2 tablespoons fish sauce, plus more as needed

2 tablespoons oyster sauce

1 tablespoon sugar, plus more as needed

450g/1lb scallops

450g/1lb mussels, scrubbed and debearded

25g/1oz/½ cup firmly packed fresh Thai basil leaves

2 Fresno chillies, deseeded and cut lengthways into narrow strips

2 Thai aubergines, quartered through the stem end (you could use baby purple aubergines if you can't find Thai)

2 tablespoons tamarind liquid (see note below)

Steamed jasmine rice for serving

Louis Tikaram, chef at E.P & L.P. in Los Angeles, puts the 'green' in green curry with this seafood-packed, wildly flavourful Thai coconut stew. When Tikaram came through the *Bong Appétit* house, he added weed in six different forms (high-cannabinoid full-spectrum extract, kief, flower rosin, CBD crystalline, THCA crystalline and fire OG flower, if you're keeping track) to make this curry pack a powerful punch, but this version doesn't require you to live *that* large. This recipe makes more curry paste than you need; freeze the extra in an ice-cube tray so you're never that far from green curry bliss.

In a medium saucepan over a high heat, combine the chicken stock, coconut cream, lime leaves and lemongrass and bring to the boil. Lower the heat to a simmer, stir in the curry paste and leave to simmer for 5 minutes to blend the flavours. Add the fish sauce, oyster sauce and sugar and stir to mix.

Add the scallops and mussels (discarding any mussels that fail to close to the touch) to the pan and cook on a gentle simmer until the mussels have begun to open and the scallops are partially cooked but still translucent in the centre, about 3 minutes. Stir in the basil, chillies and aubergines and continue to simmer until the scallops are opaque throughout and all of the mussels are open (discard any that failed to open), about 3 minutes longer. The vegetables should still be nice and firm.

Stir in the tamarind liquid and adjust the seasoning with more sugar or fish sauce, if needed. Serve hot with the rice.

Note: To make tamarind liquid, in a small bowl, soak about 3 tablespoons tamarind pulp in 125ml/4fl oz/½ cup warm water for about 15 minutes, pressing against and squeezing the pulp every now and again to soften it. Then, pour the contents of the bowl through a fine-mesh strainer placed over a second bowl and press against the solids in the strainer to force through as much of the thin purée as possible. Discard the solids. Measure what you need for the curry, then store the remainder in a tightly sealed jar in the fridge for up to 1 week.

THC
20mg per 55g/2oz/¼ cup;
240mg total recipe

Homemade Curry Paste
Makes 680g/1lb 8oz/3 cups

85g/3oz/1½ cups long, red dried chillies, deseeded

90g/3¼oz/1 cup peeled and sliced galangal

3 lemongrass stalks; grassy tops, tough outer leaves and base removed; thinly sliced

45g/1½oz/½ cup peeled and sliced turmeric root

10 garlic cloves

45g/1½oz/½ cup sliced ginger

1 tablespoon shrimp paste

3 grams cannabis flower, ground and decarboxylated (see page 54)

In a medium bowl, combine the chillies with warm water to cover and leave to soak for 20 minutes. Drain, discarding the liquid, and transfer the chillies to a blender or food processor. Add the galangal, lemongrass, turmeric root, garlic, ginger, shrimp paste and cannabis flower and process until smooth, adding a little water if needed for the blades to move freely. Transfer to an airtight container and store in the fridge for up to 1 week or in the freezer for up to 1 month.

Coconut Seafood Stew (*Moqueca*)

Natalia Pereira/Woodspoon

Serves 8

THC

11.7mg per serving;
93.6mg total recipe

With live resin:
33.7mg per serving;
293.6mg total recipe

1.3kg/3lb skinned black cod fillet, cut into 5-cm/2-inch pieces (you can use regular white cod if you can't find black)

125ml/4fl oz/½ cup olive oil

4 tablespoons freshly squeezed lime juice

3 garlic cloves, minced

Leaves and tender stems of 1 bunch coriander, coarsely chopped

2 onions, finely chopped

240ml/8fl oz/1 cup weed-infused coconut milk (see page 71)

450ml/16fl oz/2 cups coconut milk

3 tablespoons palm oil

6 tomatoes, chopped

450g/1lb large head-on prawns

1 tablespoon kosher salt or coarse sea salt

This ultra-comforting Brazilian seafood stew from chef Natalia Pereira of L.A.'s Woodspoon is called *moqueca*. Its long-simmered flavour completely belies the fact that it cooks for only 20 minutes and that the hardest thing you have to do here is infuse coconut milk. Palm oil is traditional and there isn't really a substitute; but if you can't find it, use any neutral oil instead.

In a large bowl, toss the cod with 3 tablespoons of the olive oil, 2 tablespoons of the lime juice, one-third of the garlic and half of the coriander. Let sit for 10 minutes.

Meanwhile, in a large saucepan over a medium-high heat, warm the remaining 5 tablespoons olive oil. Add the remaining garlic and the onions and cook, stirring often, until the onions are soft, about 4 minutes. Stir in both coconut milks, the palm oil and tomatoes and bring to the boil. Lower the heat to a simmer and stir in the cod and prawns. Cook until the cod is opaque throughout and the prawns have turned pink, about 8 minutes. Season with the salt, stir in the remaining coriander and serve immediately.

Vanessa Says: Coconut milk has a healthy amount of fat that is great for holding THC and flavour. At the end of the infusion, add 0.25 gram live resin to the coconut milk. Fragrant with delicate terpenes, the stew will take on a new dimension.

THC

18mg per serving;
108mg total recipe

Confit Octopus

MUNCHIES Test Kitchen
Serves 6

1 x 1.8kg/4lb octopus, cleaned (ask your fishmonger do this for you)

Kosher salt or coarse sea salt

2 garlic cloves, smashed

1 bunch oregano, plus
2 tablespoons oregano leaves for serving

125ml/4fl oz/½ cup canola oil

450ml/16fl oz/2 cups olive oil

4 tablespoons flower-infused olive oil (see page 64)

3 tablespoons red wine vinegar

15 Castelvetrano (Nocellara del Belice) olives, stoned and lightly crushed

3 celery sticks, thinly sliced on the diagonal

1 small red onion, thinly sliced

1 x 400g/14oz can chickpeas, drained and rinsed

Freshly ground black pepper

We know octopus can look a little intimidating, even if you're *not* high. All those tentacles. All those suction cups. But octopus has a secret: it's actually wildly easy to cook. You put it in some liquid, let it cook low and slow, forget about it for a while, and then you come back and it's perfect. MUNCHIES' own Action Bronson is a big fan of dabbing while waiting for his octopus to be done, but since you're poaching this guy in infused olive oil, you don't even need to. But that's not to say you can't. We're not going to tell you how to live your life.

Season the octopus tentacles with salt and place in a large saucepan along with the garlic, oregano bunch, canola oil, regular olive oil and 2 tablespoons of the infused olive oil. Bring to a low simmer, uncovered, over a medium heat and cook until tender, about 1 hour. The octopus is ready when a knife tip slides easily into the thickest part of a tentacle. Using tongs, transfer the octopus to a chopping board, leave to cool until it can be handled, then cut the tentacles on the diagonal into 1-cm/½-inch pieces and transfer to a bowl.

Let the tentacles cool to room temperature. Add the remaining 2 tablespoons infused oil, vinegar, olives, celery, onion and chickpeas and toss to mix. Season with salt and pepper, add the oregano leaves and toss again. Transfer to a platter and serve immediately.

Desserts

THC
5mg per truffle;
160mg total recipe

Truffles

Vanessa Lavorato

Makes 32 truffles

450g/5oz/1 cup finely chopped good-quality dark chocolate (66% cacao)

5 tablespoons weed-infused cream (see page 72)

3 tablespoons double cream

1 tablespoon bourbon

1 tablespoon honey

1 pinch kosher salt or coarse sea salt

1 tablespoon unsalted butter, at room temperature

⅛ teaspoon vanilla extract

100g/3½oz/1 cup cocoa powder

Imagine how sick it would be to show up to someone's party with a box of these. 'Oh, it's nothing. Just a box of bud-and-bourbon-infused chocolate truffles I made myself.' You'd be invited literally everywhere after that. Bourbon is Vanessa's all-time favourite alcohol in the kitchen. Use a good bourbon and a dark chocolate here. The honey complements the liquor and adds a nice shine to the ganache. These truffles make the perfect host gift that is sure to be the highlight of the night. Vanessa microdoses them for a reason; *non c'è due senza tre* is italian for 'betcha can't eat just one.'

Place the chocolate in a small metal bowl.

In a small saucepan over a medium heat, combine both creams, the bourbon, honey and salt. Cook, stirring constantly, until the cream just starts to bubble. Pour the warm cream over the chocolate and leave to sit for 5 minutes.

Using a rubber spatula, stir the mixture slowly, working in small circles from the centre and moving outwards, until all the ingredients are incorporated and the chocolate has melted. Once the mixture reaches 35°C/95°F on an instant-read thermometer, add the butter and vanilla and stir well to combine. Refrigerate the ganache for about 2 hours, until firm.

Place the cocoa powder in a large bowl.

Roll, scoop, or pipe the ganache into 1-teaspoon balls. Toss the balls in the cocoa powder to coat completely. Transfer to an airtight container and store in the fridge for up to 1 week.

THC
1.1mg per piece;
66.8mg total recipe

Stoner Marshmallow Bites

Thu Tran
Makes 60 pieces

115g/4oz/2 cups crushed crisps
(we recommend Kettle Chips
with sea salt)

140g/5oz/2 cups crushed
pretzels

115g/4oz/2 cups crushed
corn flakes

4 tablespoons flower-infused
butter (see page 68)

85g/3oz/2 cups mini
marshmallows

640g/1lb 7oz/4 cups dark
chocolate chips

225g/8oz unsweetened dark
chocolate (95–99% cacao),
coarsely chopped

4 tablespoons sprinkles
(optional)

Maldon sea salt (optional)

Vanessa Says: Add a tablespoon of
infused coconut oil to the chocolate.
It will make the chocolate thinner
and easier to work with as well as
up the dose.

Thu Tran is the delightful creative genius behind *Food Party*, a show
that blends cooking with puppets, interactive snacks and pure
unadulterated weirdness. It's an amazing thing to watch when you're
high. And since you're already high, you may as well be eating this,
the finest stoner snack known to man – sweet, salty, chocolatey,
crunchy and chewy, all in one tiny package.

Line a 23 by 33-cm/9 by 13-inch baking tray with baking parchment
and set aside. In a large bowl, combine the crisps, pretzels and corn
flakes and set aside.

In a medium saucepan over a medium heat, melt the infused butter.
Add the marshmallows and cook, stirring, until melted and smooth,
about 5 minutes. Pour the marshmallow-butter mixture over the
crisps mixture and stir to mix well. Transfer the mixture to the
prepared baking tray and spread in an even layer, pressing it to
flatten. Refrigerate for about 30 minutes, until cool.

Pour water to a depth of 5cm/2 inches in a medium saucepan and
bring to a gentle simmer over a low heat. Put the chocolate chips
and dark chocolate in a heatproof bowl and set the bowl over (not
touching) the water in the saucepan. Heat, stirring, until the chocolate
has melted and is smooth.

Spread the warm chocolate over the mixture in the pan. Top with the
sprinkles or a scattering of sea salt, if desired. Refrigerate, uncovered,
until cooled completely. Cut the potato chip-marshmallow mixture
into 60 pieces. Transfer to an airtight container and store in the
fridge for up to 5 days.

THC
6mg per ice pop;
66.8mg total recipe

With infused cream:
18mg per ice pop;
200.6mg total recipe

Frozen Cocoa Pudding Pops

KELLY FIELDS/WILLA JEAN

Makes 11 ice pops

290ml/10fl oz/1¼ cups double cream, plus 60ml/2fl oz/¼ cup regular or weed-infused cream (see page 72)

350ml/12fl oz/1½ cups whole milk

½ vanilla pod, split lengthways

100g/3½oz/½ cup sugar

2 tablespoons cocoa powder

Kosher salt or coarse sea salt

2 large eggs

4 tablespoons flower-infused butter (see page 68), at room temperature, cubed

115g/4oz dark chocolate (70% cacao; we recommend Valrhona brand), coarsely chopped

Kelly Fields, chef and partner at Willa Jean in New Orleans, may or may not be the person who invented frozen rosé – the history is hazy, and there are a lot of pretenders to the throne; for the record, we believe her. But she's definitely the person who came up with the equally brilliant idea of putting drugs in Fudgsicles. If you don't have ice-lolly moulds, you can just freeze the base in a plastic container and scoop it like ice cream, keeping in mind that the dosage will change depending on the size of the scoops.

In a medium, heavy saucepan over a medium-high heat, combine the double cream, milk and vanilla pod and warm just to scalding (tiny bubbles begin to form along the sides of the pan).

Meanwhile, in a medium bowl, whisk together the sugar, cocoa powder and 2 teaspoons salt. Add the eggs and whisk until smooth.

When the cream-milk mixture is ready, remove it from the heat. Add about 60ml/2fl oz/¼ cup of the hot liquid to the egg-sugar mixture while whisking constantly. Continue whisking in the hot liquid, 60ml/2fl oz/¼ cup at a time, until most of the hot liquid is incorporated into the egg mixture. Then whisk the cream-egg mixture into cream mixture remaining in the saucepan and place over a medium heat. Cook, whisking constantly, until the mixture thickens and bubbles, about 5 minutes. Remove from the heat and immediately whisk in the infused butter and chocolate until melted.

Remove and discard the vanilla pod. Taste and adjust with salt, if needed. Leave to cool slightly, pour into 90-ml/3-fl oz ice-lolly moulds and freeze until set. Store in the freezer for up to 1 month.

THC

14.8mg per serving;
133.8mg total recipe

With whipped weed-infused
honey: 18.8mg per serving;
171.2mg total recipe

Honey Rosemary Ice Cream

Mindy Segal
Makes 9 servings

450ml/16fl oz/2 cups whole milk

400ml/14fl oz/1¾ cups double cream

60ml/2fl oz/¼ cup weed-infused cream (see page 72)

4 rosemary sprigs, stems removed and reserved and leaves coarsely chopped

200g/7oz/1 cup sugar

13 egg yolks

125ml/4fl oz/½ cup whipped weed-infused honey (see page 74; optional)

1 teaspoon vanilla extract

½ teaspoon kosher salt or coarse sea salt

Mindy Segal is a pastry chef and cookie genius who was among the first serious chefs to get into commercial edibles. She's elevated the use of cannabis in sweets to an art form, an accomplishment that's clear on first taste of this herby-sweet ice cream. Use a strain high in pinene, like Northern Lights, in your infused cream to play up the rosemary, or swap in some whipped infused honey to play up the get-you-baked-ness.

In a medium saucepan over a medium-low heat, combine the milk, both creams and rosemary leaves and stems and warm for 1 hour. Ensure the mixture does not boil or scald. You are simply infusing over a low heat at this stage.

Meanwhile, in a large bowl, whisk the sugar and egg yolks until blended. When the cream mixture is ready, bring it just to the boil, remove from the heat, and slowly pour it into yolk mixture while whisking constantly until fully combined. Pour the mixture back into the saucepan and cook over a medium heat, stirring constantly, until thick, about 25 minutes.

Remove the pan from the heat and stir in the honey (if using), vanilla and salt. Leave to cool for several minutes, then cover and refrigerate until cold.

Strain the mixture through a fine-mesh strainer set over a bowl. Transfer to an ice-cream maker and freeze according to the manufacturer's instructions. Scoop into an airtight container, transfer to the freezer and store for up to 1 month.

THC

5.5mg per brownie;
66.8mg total recipe

With infused peanut butter
sauce and infused whipped
cream: 26.2mg per serving;
310.6mg total recipe

For the Brownies

6 tablespoons flower-infused butter (see page 68)

4 tablespoons unsalted butter

115g/4oz dark chocolate (70% cacao; we recommend Valrhona brand), coarsely chopped

115g/4oz semi-sweet chocolate (around 50% cacao), coarsely chopped

2 large eggs

200g/7oz/1 cup sugar

2 teaspoons vanilla extract

¼ teaspoon kosher salt or coarse sea salt

120g/4¼oz/scant 1 cup plain flour, sifted

For the Peanut Butter Sauce

335g/11¾oz/1½ cups Homemade Peanut Butter (see page 232)

400g/14oz/2 cups sugar

240ml/8fl oz/1 cup water

For Serving

Vanilla ice cream

Whipped Weed-Infused Cream (page 73)

Chocolate sauce

Sugar sprinkles

Maraschino cherries

Vanessa Says: Infuse the whipped cream with a fragrant variety like Forbidden Fruit for a THC cherry on top of your sundae.

Brownie Sundae

MUNCHIES TEST KITCHEN
Makes 12 sundaes

At this point, is there a single recipe more clichéd than the pot brownie? But it seemed wrong not to include one. Eat it as is and revel in your basicness, or put it in a sundae with ice cream, weed-laced peanut butter sauce, chocolate sauce, whipped infused cream, sprinkles and a cherry – because you're worth it.

To make the brownies: Heat the oven to 180°C fan/200°C/400°F/ gas 6. Grease a 23 by 33-cm/9 by 13-inch baking tin, line with baking parchment and then grease the parchment. Set aside.

Pour water to a depth of 5cm/2 inches in a medium saucepan and bring to a simmer. Put both butters and both chocolates in a heatproof bowl and set the bowl over (not touching) the water in the saucepan. Heat, stirring, until the mixture is melted and smooth, about 5 minutes. Remove from the heat and set aside.

In a medium bowl, whisk the eggs until blended. Add the sugar, vanilla and salt and whisk until incorporated. Stir in the chocolate mixture, mixing well, and then fold in the flour until no white streaks remain. Transfer to the prepared tin, spreading evenly.

Bake until a thin skin forms on top and a cocktail stick inserted into the centre comes out with a few moist crumbs clinging to it, about 18 to 20 minutes. Transfer the tin to a wire rack to cool completely. Cut into twelve 8 by 10-cm/3 by 4-inch brownies. Transfer to an airtight container and store at room temperature for up to 5 days.

To make the peanut butter sauce: In a small saucepan over a medium-low heat, combine the peanut butter, sugar and water and cook, stirring, until the peanut butter and sugar melt and the sauce is smooth, about 5 minutes. Remove from the heat and leave to cool. Transfer to an airtight container and store in the fridge for up to 1 week. Reheat gently before serving.

For each serving, place a brownie in a bowl or sundae glass. Top with a scoop of ice cream, a heaped tablespoon whipped cream, 3 tablespoons of the peanut butter sauce, as much chocolate sauce as you like, a scattering of sprinkles and a cherry.

THC
3.7mg per cookie;
66.8mg total recipe

Salted Chocolate Chip Cookies

MUNCHIES Test Kitchen

Makes 18 cookies

225g/8oz/1¾ cups plain flour

¾ teaspoon bicarbonate of soda

½ teaspoon kosher salt or coarse sea salt

4 tablespoons flower-infused butter (see page 68), at room temperature

4 tablespoons unsalted butter, at room temperature

2 tablespoons sugar

200g/7oz/1 cup light brown sugar

1 large egg

½ vanilla pod, split lengthways

225g/8oz semi-sweet chocolate (about 50% cacao), coarsely chopped

Maldon sea salt

Vanessa Says: You can also swap a already-infused chocolate bar for the chocolate in this recipe. Chop it up, keeping in mind the milligrams, to get you to the right dose.

Everyone needs one perfect chocolate chip cookie recipe in their arsenal, and it may as well be one that gets you blazed. Chopping the chocolate into irregular chunks (use a serrated knife for that) ensures there's a bit of chocolate in every bite.

Line two baking trays with baking parchment and set aside.

In a medium bowl, stir together the flour, bicarbonate of soda and kosher salt. In a large bowl, combine both butters and beat with a wooden spoon until soft and smooth. Add both sugars to the butter and beat until the mixture is lighter in colour and fluffy. Add the egg and beat until incorporated. Using the tip of a knife, scrape the seeds from the vanilla pod, add to the bowl and stir to mix well. Add the flour mixture and stir just until fully incorporated, then fold in the chocolate.

Divide the dough into 18 equal portions, shape each portion into a ball and arrange the balls on the prepared baking trays, spacing them about 5cm/2 inches apart. Sprinkle each ball with a healthy pinch of Maldon salt, then refrigerate, uncovered, for 2 hours.

Heat the oven to 170°C fan/190°C/375°F/gas 5.

Bake the cookies, directly from the fridge, until set on the outside but still soft in the middle, about 10 minutes. Remove from the oven and transfer the cookies to a wire rack to cool slightly. Transfer to an airtight container and store at room temperature for up to 1 week.

THC
8.4mg per slice;
66.8mg total recipe

Raspberry and Peach Pie

TRACY OBOLSKY/ROCKAWAY BEACH BAKERY
Serves 8

For the Pastry Case

400g/14oz/3 cups plain flour

3½ teaspoons sugar

¾ teaspoon kosher salt or
coarse sea salt

125ml/4fl oz/½ cup cold
flower-infused butter
(see page 68), cubed

115g/4oz/½ cup cold unsalted
butter, cubed

55g/2oz/¼ cup shortening,
frozen and cut into chunks

170ml/5½fl oz/scant ¾ cup
ice-cold water

1 egg, plus 1 egg yolk

For the Oat Crumble

125g/4oz/½ cup plus
1 tablespoon unsalted butter

½ teaspoon vanilla extract

170g/6oz/1¼ cups plain flour

100g/3½oz/1 cup old-fashioned
rolled oats

200g/7oz/1 cup sugar

½ teaspoon kosher salt or
coarse sea salt

Tracy Obolsky runs New York's Rockaway Beach Bakery, a sick bakery out in Queens where she's basically the queen of putting butter in things (her croissant game is top-notch). So it's not shocking that her pastry case is impeccable – whether it involves infused butter or not. This pie showcases her skills on all counts: juicy filling, tender oat-crumble topping and a flaky, shattery crust that also gets you high. Just remember that half of the dough is being saved for a second pastry case; so if you use it all for a double-crust pie, the total THC would be about 133.6mg.

To make the pastry case: In a large bowl, stir together the flour, sugar and salt. Scatter both butters over the top and, using your fingers, mix the butters with the flour until pea-sized crumbles form. Add the shortening and mix again to form small crumbles. Drizzle the water over the flour mixture, lifting and turning the mixture as you go so the water is evenly distributed and a shaggy dough begins to form. Do not overmix. Press the dough into a rough mass, then divide it in half. You will need only half of the dough for this recipe. Flatten each half into a disk about 2.5cm/1 inch thick. Wrap one disk in cling film and refrigerate for 1 hour to use for this pie. Double wrap the remaining disk and freeze for up to 1 month; defrost overnight in the fridge before using.

Grease a 23-cm/9-inch pie plate.

On a lightly floured surface, roll out the dough into a 30-cm/12-inch round. Transfer the dough round to the prepared pie plate, pressing it gently onto the bottom and sides. Trim away the excess dough, leaving a roughly 2-cm/¾-inch overhang. Turn the overhang under itself and then flute the edge or press the edge with a floured fork. Refrigerate for 30 minutes.

continued

Raspberry and Peach Pie, *continued*

For the Filling

2 large fresh peaches, cut into 1-cm/½-inch pieces

100g/3½oz/¾ cup raspberries

2 tablespoons demerara sugar

3½ teaspoons sugar

2½ teaspoons cornflour

2 teaspoons plain flour

2 teaspoons freshly squeezed lemon juice

Heat the oven to 160°C fan/180°C/350°F/gas 4.

Line the pastry case with baking parchment and fill with baking beans. Bake until the crust is set and the edges are lightly browned, about 45 minutes. Remove from the oven and remove the baking beans and parchment.

In a small bowl, whisk together the egg and egg yolk until blended, then brush the bottom, sides and edge of the crust with the beaten egg. Return the crust to the oven and bake until golden and firm, about 20 minutes longer. Transfer to a wire rack and leave to cool completely. You can bake the crust up to a day in advance and then wrap it well and store at room temperature.

To make the oat crumble: In a small saucepan over a low heat, warm the butter with the vanilla just until the butter melts, then remove from the heat.

In a medium bowl, stir together the flour, oats, sugar and salt. Pour the butter mixture into the flour mixture and mix with loose fingertips just until small crumbles form. Transfer to a baking tray, spread in a thin layer, and chill until firm, about 20 minutes. The crumble can be transferred to a ziplock bag and refrigerated for up to 5 days or frozen for up to 1 month.

Heat the oven to 150°C fan/170°C/325°F/gas 3.

To make the filling: In a large bowl, combine the peaches, raspberries, brown sugar, sugar, cornflour, plain flour and lemon juice and stir to mix evenly.

Spoon the filling into the baked pastry case, then top evenly with the oat crumble.

Bake the pie until the crumble is golden and the filling is bubbling, about 1 hour. Transfer to a wire rack and leave to cool slightly. The pie will keep, covered, in the fridge for up to 5 days. Serve warm or at room temperature.

THC
13.4mg per serving;
133.8mg total recipe

Strawberry Shortcake Trifle

MUNCHIES Test Kitchen

Serves 10

12 egg whites

1 teaspoon kosher salt or coarse sea salt

200g/7oz/1 granulated cup sugar

3 teaspoons vanilla extract

120g/4½oz/scant 1 cup plain flour

140g/5oz/1 cup icing sugar

850g/1lb 12oz/6 cups thinly sliced strawberries

350ml/12fl oz/1½ cups double cream

125ml/4fl oz/½ cup weed-infused cream (see page 72)

Angel food cake is super-hard to get weed into because it is so delicate and low in fat. So instead, we've worked the weed into a strawberry shortcake-inspired trifle. This layered confection has delicate cake, sweet juicy strawberries and weed-loaded whipped cream. Source a strain of weed full of ripe berry notes, like Strawberry Haze or Strawberry Cough, to make your infused cream (and to roll into a joint to pair with your dessert). If you don't feel like spooning from a trifle bowl, layer in individual glasses.

Heat the oven to 150°C fan/170°C/325°F/gas 3.

In a large bowl, using a handheld mixer on medium speed, beat the egg whites and salt until foamy, then increase the speed to medium-high and beat until soft peaks form. Gradually add 130g/4½oz/ ⅔ cup of the granulated sugar and continue beating until stiff peaks form. Stir in 2 teaspoons of the vanilla until evenly mixed.

In a medium bowl, stir together the flour and 90g/3¼oz/⅔ cup of the icing sugar. With the mixer on low speed, gradually add one-third of the flour mixture to the egg whites and mix just until incorporated. Repeat with the remaining flour mixture in two equal batches, again mixing just until incorporated after each addition. Pour the batter into a 25-cm/10-inch tube cake tin, then bang the tin lightly on the counter to remove any air pockets.

Bake the cake until golden on top and a cake tester or cocktail stick inserted into the centre comes out clean, about 25 to 30 minutes.

Remove the cake from the oven and invert the tin to cool. (Most tube tins have small feet attached to the rim, so the tin will stand clear of the work surface when inverted. If your tin doesn't, you will need to improvise. For example, slipping the tube over the neck of a wine bottle works.) Let the cake stand until cooled completely, about 1 hour. Slide a knife around the sides and centre tube of the tin to loosen the cake sides, then gently remove the cake from the tin.

continued

Vanessa Says: For added flavour and a boozy kick, macerate the strawberries in weed tequila (see Nitrous Green Dragon, page 77) before adding them to the trifle, or drizzle the fruit with a little of the glycerine-based cannabis tincture on page 83 for some extra THC.

Strawberry Shortcake Trifle, *continued*

In a medium bowl, toss the strawberries with the remaining granulated sugar. Leave to sit for 15 minutes, stirring occasionally.

In a large bowl, combine both creams, the remaining icing sugar and remaining 1 teaspoon vanilla. Using the handheld mixer or a whisk, beat until the cream is thick and silky. Cover and refrigerate until ready to use, up to 1 day.

Tear the cake into 2.5-cm/1-inch pieces. Layer one-third of the cake pieces on the bottom of a trifle bowl and top with one-third of the whipped cream. Drizzle with some of the strawberry juice, then spoon about one-third of the strawberries on top. Repeat the layering until you have three layers each of cake, whipped cream and strawberries. Cover and refrigerate (up to overight), then use a large spoon to serve.

THC

8.9mg per slice;
71.2mg total recipe

With weed-infused coconut oil
in the crust: 13.4mg per slice;
106.8mg total recipe

Strawberry 'Cheesecake'

Jasmine Shimoda
Serves 8

For the Crust

260g/9¼oz/2 cups skin-on
raw almonds

10 Medjool dates, stoned

2 tablespoons coconut oil or
flower-infused coconut oil
(see page 64)

2 tablespoons raw
cacao powder

1 tablespoon kosher salt or
coarse sea salt

For the Filling

200g/7oz/2 cups strawberries,
hulled

350g/12oz/3 cups raw cashews,
soaked in water to cover
overnight, then drained
and rinsed

115g/4oz/1 cup dried goji
berries or dried cherries

185g/6oz/¾ cup maple syrup

60ml/2fl oz/¼ cup freshly
squeezed lemon juice

60g/2oz/¼ cup coconut butter

60ml/2fl oz/¼ cup flower-
infused coconut oil
(see page 64)

This is another banger from yogi chef Jasmine Shimoda (see her inspired kale salad on page 124). It's a gluten-free, dairy-free, raw 'cheesecake' that is (a) full of weed and (b) genuinely enjoyable. If you can't find sweet-tart goji berries, dried cherries work fine, but the internet works better. A whole fan leaf placed on the top when serving will make the presentation iconic.

To make the crust: Put the almonds in a food processor and pulse until reduced to a fine powder. Add the dates, coconut oil, cacao powder and salt and process until the dough comes together to form a ball. Transfer the dough to a 23-cm/9-inch springform cake tin and press evenly onto the bottom. Cover with cling film and refrigerate for 1 hour.

To make the filling: Place the strawberries in a blender and process until smooth. Add the cashews, goji berries, maple syrup and lemon juice and process again until smooth. Finally, add the coconut butter and infused coconut oil and process until smooth.

Pour the filling into the cake tin, spreading it evenly over the crust, then cover tightly and freeze for 24 hours. (The cake will keep in the freezer for up to 1 month before serving.)

Release and lift off the sides of the tin and slide the cake onto a serving plate. Leave to soften slightly in the fridge for 1 hour before serving. Any leftovers will keep in the fridge for up to 5 days.

Pro Tip: See if you can find a Goji Berry OG Kush strain by Bodhi to make this super soigné.

THC

17.5mg per serving;
72mg total recipe

With cannabis flower:
19.9mg per serving;
81.5mg total recipe

300g/10½oz/1½ cups firmly packed light brown sugar

3 tablespoons flower-infused butter (see page 68)

0.5 gram raw kief

½ teaspoon kosher salt or coarse sea salt

4 bananas, peeled, halved lengthways and then halved crossways into 16 pieces

3 grams cannabis flower (optional)

60ml/2fl oz/¼ cup Cognac (preferably Hennessy)

Vanilla ice cream for serving

Bananas Foster

MUNCHIES TEST KITCHEN
Serves 4

Classic Bananas Foster is already a fairly dramatic dish, what with the lighting things on fire and all. This version adds a little extra drama with infused butter and kief. And if you're fully prepared to live large, warm some fat nugs in the butter with the bananas and get it all real smoky.

In a 30-cm/12-inch frying over a medium-low heat, combine the brown sugar, infused butter, kief and salt and cook, stirring, until the sugar dissolves in the butter. Add the bananas and cannabis flower (if using) and cook, stirring gently every now and again, until the bananas are soft, about 10 minutes.

Add the Cognac, let it heat briefly, and then, working carefully, ignite the Cognac with a long match or a fire starter. Continue to cook until the flames die out. Serve immediately with ice cream.

THC
5mg per gummy;
450mg total recipe

After-Dinner Mint Gummies

Anna Posey/Elske

Makes 90 gummies

Vegetable oil for greasing

70g/2½oz/½ cup icing sugar

50g/1¾oz/½ cup cornflour

510ml/17½fl oz/generous
2 cups water

24 sheets silver gelatine

1½ teaspoons food-grade
eucalyptus extract

½ teaspoon spearmint extract

½ teaspoon matcha powder

¼ teaspoon spirulina powder

625ml/22fl oz/2⅔ cups
liquid sucrose

1 tablespoon liquid glucose

170ml/5½fl oz/scant ¾ cup
glycerine cannabis tincture
(see page 83)

2 egg whites

Think of this as a super-classy after-dinner mint that refreshes your palate *and* gets you high (and it gets its colour from spirulina, so it can probably cure your cold, too). Pastry chef Anna Posey, of Elske in Chicago, is known for her restrained, delicate nature-inspired desserts, and this deep, deep green eucalyptus-and-mint jelly is no exception. You'll need to hunt down some of the ingredients – stopping at speciality baking suppliers and natural food stores, or the internet for the whole lot – but these sweets are worth the trouble.

Line a 23 by 33-cm/9 by 13-inch baking tray with baking parchment, then grease the parchment with vegetable oil.

In a small bowl, stir together the icing sugar and cornflour, mixing well. Dust the prepared tray evenly with a quarter of the mixture, then set aside.

Pour half of the water into a small saucepan, immerse the gelatine in the water, and let sit until soft, about 5 minutes. Place the pan over a medium-low heat and warm just until the gelatine melts, then stir in the eucalyptus extract, spearmint extract, matcha and spirulina. Remove from the heat and set aside.

In a second small saucepan, stir together the sucrose, glucose, tincture and remaining water. Place over a medium heat and warm without stirring to 126°C/260°F on a deep-frying thermometer. (It is important not to stir while heating as it can cause crystallisation.) Remove from the heat, whisk the gelatine mixture into the syrup mixture and set aside.

Meanwhile, in a medium bowl, whisk the egg whites until frothy. While continuously whisking (by hand or with a handheld mixer), gradually pour the gelatine-syrup mixture in a slow, steady stream into the egg whites. Take care to pour the hot syrup directly into the egg whites, being careful it does not hit the whisk first and splash against the sides of the bowl. (If the syrup spatters, it will adhere to the bowl sides.) Continue to whisk until the mixture has thickened slightly.

Pour the mixture into the prepared tray in an even layer. Dust with another quarter of the icing sugar mixture and leave to sit at room temperature until set, for about 3 hours.

Dust a chopping board with about 2 tablespoons of the icing sugar mixture. Cut the gummy sheet into ninety 2.5 by 3.5cm/1 by 1⅓ inch pieces, then remove the pieces from the pan and roll them in the remaining icing sugar mixture, dusting off any excess. Transfer to an airtight container and store at room temperature for up to 2 weeks.

Adult Celebration Cake

MICHELLE GAYER/SALTY TART
Serves 16

This towering, cream-stuffed, Froot Loops-packed cake from Michelle Gayer of Minneapolis bakery Salty Tart is kind of a brainteaser for the stoner cook: We see at least five places (twice in the cake batter, once in the buttercream, twice in the filling) where you can sneak in some weed. Can you find any others?

	THC IN MILLIGRAMS	
	Per Slice	Total Recipe
With weed-infused olive oil	14.5	233
With weed-infused butter	20.8	334
With weed-infused olive oil and weed-infused butter	35	560

For the Cake

240ml/8fl oz/1 cup olive oil, regular or flower-infused (see page 64)

240ml/8fl oz/1 cup soured cream

285g/10oz/1¼ cups butter, unsalted or flower-infused (see page 68), at room temperature

650g/1lb 7oz/5 cups plain flour

700g/1lb 9oz/3½ cups sugar

40g/1½oz/¼ cup baking powder

1½ teaspoons kosher salt or coarse sea salt

700ml/26fl oz/3 cups whole milk

7 eggs, lightly beaten

30g/1oz/1 cup Froot Loops cereal, chopped, plus extra for sprinkling

Heat the oven to 160°C fan/180°C/350°F/gas 4. Grease three 20-cm/8-inch round cake tins, then line the bottoms with baking parchment.

In a food mixer fitted with the paddle attachment, combine the olive oil, soured cream and butter. Top with the flour, sugar, baking powder and salt. Mix on medium speed just until a crumbly consistency forms. In a medium bowl, whisk together the milk and eggs until blended. With the mixer on low speed, slowly add the milk-egg mixture in three equal additions, mixing until fully combined and scraping down the sides of the bowl after each addition. With the mixer still on low speed, add the cereal and mix just until combined. Divide the batter evenly among the prepared cake tins.

Bake the cakes until a knife inserted into the centre of one comes out clean, about 55 minutes. Transfer to wire racks and leave to cool for about 20 minutes. Run a knife blade around the inside edge of a tin to loosen the cake sides, invert the cake onto a rack, lift off the tin, peel off the parchment and turn the layer right-side up. Repeat with

continued

Adult Celebration Cake, *continued*

the remaining cakes and leave to cool completely. The cakes can be well wrapped and stored at room temperature for up to 3 days or in the freezer for up to 1 month; defrost overnight in the fridge.

	THC IN MILLIGRAMS	
	Per Slice	Total Recipe
With weed-infused butter	6.3	100

For the Buttercream

650g/1lb 7oz/3¼ cups sugar

14 egg whites

900g/2lb/4 cups unsalted butter, plus 85g/3oz/ 6 tablespoons, unsalted or flower-infused (see page 68), at room temperature

6 tablespoons hot water

1 teaspoon kosher salt or coarse sea salt

Grated zest of 1 lemon

Pour water to a depth of 2.5cm/1 inch into a 4-litre/7-pint saucepan and bring to a simmer over a medium heat. Put the sugar and egg whites in a large heatproof bowl and set the bowl over (not touching) the water in the saucepan. Heat, stirring, until the sugar has dissolved into the egg whites, about 10 minutes.

Transfer the egg white-sugar mixture to the food mixer fitted with the whisk attachment and whisk on medium-high speed until cool and thick. Add the butter and continue to whisk until creamy and thick. Add the hot water, salt and lemon zest and whisk until fully incorporated, about 3 minutes longer. Cover and refrigerate for up to 1 week.

	THC IN MILLIGRAMS	
	Per Slice	Total Recipe
With weed-infused cream	33.4	535
Wwith whipped weed-infused honey	1.6	56
With weed-infused cream and whipped weed-infused honey	35	560˙

For the Whipped Cream Filling

240ml/8fl oz/1 cup double cream, plus 240ml/8fl oz/1 cup double cream or weed-infused cream (see page 72)

240ml/8fl oz/1 cup soured cream

185ml/6fl oz/¾ cup whipped honey, regular or weed-infused (see page 74)

1 pinch kosher salt or coarse sea salt

In the food mixer fitted with the whisk attachment, combine the cream, soured cream, honey and salt and whisk on high speed until thick and fluffy, about 5 to 8 minutes. Cover and refrigerate for up to 3 days.

Using a long, serrated knife in a sawing motion, horizontally split each cake into three layers. To make it easier to cut, freeze the cakes for about 2 hours before cutting into thirds. You will have a total of nine layers.

Set a cake layer on a cake plate or stand. Spoon about one-quarter of the buttercream into a piping bag fitted with a 1-cm/½-inch plain tip and pipe a narrow wall around the edge of the layer (this is a 'fence' to keep the cream filling in place). Fill the centre with about 125g/4oz/½ cup of the whipped cream filling, spreading it in an even layer with a palette knife. Top with a second cake layer and repeat the fence and filling. Continue in this way until you have stacked and filled eight layers. Top with the final cake layer and, using the palette knife, spread a thin layer of buttercream over the top and sides of the cake to seal in any loose crumbs, creating a smooth surface. Refrigerate the cake for about 30 minutes to set the crumb coat.

To finish, mound about one-third of the remaining buttercream on top of the cake and, using broad, smooth strokes, spread it evenly. Then, working in batches, apply the remaining buttercream to the sides of the cake in an even layer, returning to the top once again to smooth any rough edges. Sprinkle the top with Froot Loops. The cake will keep, covered, in the fridge, for up to 5 days. Cut into even slices to serve.

Choose-Your-Own-Adventure Assembly

	THC IN MILLIGRAMS	
	Per Slice	Total Recipe
Buttercream with weed-infused butter and Filling with weed-infused cream	39.6	635
Buttercream with weed-infused butter and Filling with whipped weed-infused honey	7.8	125.6
Buttercream with weed-infused butter and Filling with weed-infused cream and whipped weed-infused honey	41.3	660

	THC IN MILLIGRAMS	
	Per Slice	Total Recipe
Cake with weed-infused olive oil and Buttercream with weed-infused butter	20.8	333
Cake with weed-infused butter and Buttercream with weed-infused butter	27	434
Cake with weed-infused olive oil and weed-infused butter and Buttercream with weed-infused butter	41.6	665

Vanessa Says: A cake of this measure deserves the appropriate accessories. Candied cannabis leaves are crunchy and sweet. Lay smaller fan leaves on a parchment-lined baking tray and paint them with a 3:1 sugar-to-water sugar syrup. Place in a an oven at 100°C fan/120°C/240°F/gas ½ for 10 minutes (ideally with convection; it'll take a little longer without), until glossy and dry.

continued

Adult Celebration Cake, *continued*

	THC IN MILLIGRAMS	
	Per Slice	Total Recipe
Cake with weed-infused olive oil and Filling with weed-infused cream	47.9	766
Cake with weed-infused olive oil and Filling with whipped weed-infused honey	16	257
Cake with weed-infused olive oil and Filling with weed-infused cream and whipped weed-infused honey	50	790

	THC IN MILLIGRAMS	
	Per Slice	Total Recipe
Cake with weed-infused butter and Filling with weed-infused cream	54	867
Cake with weed-infused butter and Filling with whipped weed-infused honey	22.4	358
Cake with weed-infused butter and Filling with weed-infused cream and whipped weed-infused honey	55.6	889.6

	THC IN MILLIGRAMS	
	Per Slice	Total Recipe
Cake with weed-infused olive oil and weed-infused butter and Filling with weed-infused cream	68.7	1,099
Cake with weed-infused olive oil and weed-infused butter and Filling with whipped weed-infused honey	37	590
Cake with weed-infused olive oil and weed-infused butter and Filling with weed-infused cream and whipped weed-infused honey	70	1,125

	THC IN MILLIGRAMS	
	Per Slice	Total Recipe
Cake with weed-infused olive oil, Buttercream with weed-infused butter and Filling with weed-infused cream	54	864
Cake with weed-infused olive oil, Buttercream with weed-infused butter and Filling with whipped weed-infused honey	22.4	357
Cake with weed-infused olive oil, Buttercream with weed-infused butter and Filling with weed-infused cream and whipped weed-infused honey	55.7	892

	THC IN MILLIGRAMS	
	Per Slice	Total Recipe
Cake with weed-infused butter, Buttercream with weed-infused butter and Filling with weed-infused cream	60	967
Cake with weed-infused butter, Buttercream with weed-infused butter and Filling with whipped weed-infused honey	28.6	458
Cake with weed-infused butter, Buttercream with weed-infused butter and Filling with weed-infused cream and whipped weed-infused honey	61.6	985

	THC IN MILLIGRAMS	
	Per Slice	Total Recipe
Cake with weed-infused olive oil and weed-infused butter, Buttercream with weed-infused butter and Filling with weed-infused cream	75	1,200
Cake with weed-infused olive oil and weed-infused butter, Buttercream with weed-infused butter and Filling with whipped weed-infused honey	43	688
Cake with weed-infused olive oil and weed-infused butter, Buttercream with weed-infused butter and Filling with weed-infused cream and whipped weed-infused honey	76.5	1,225

Projects

THC
20.8mg per 55g/2oz/¼ cup;
83.2mg total recipe

Cannabis Leaf Pesto

MUNCHIES Test Kitchen
Makes 225g/8oz/1 cup

4 cannabis fan leaves

65g/2¼oz/1½ cups basil leaves

65g/2¼oz/¼ cup pine nuts, toasted

40g/1½oz/½ cup grated Parmesan cheese

125ml/4fl oz/½ cup flower-infused olive oil (see page 64)

Kosher salt or coarse sea salt

Much as in the chimichurri on page 157, weed leaves add vegetal vibes to this classic pesto. If you want to make things extra soigné, chilling the olive oil for half an hour in the fridge before adding it to the pesto helps the leaves stay nice and green while they're being pulverised.

In a food processor, combine the cannabis leaves, basil, pine nuts, cheese and infused olive oil and process until the leaves are finely chopped. Season with salt. Use right away, or transfer to an airtight container and store in the fridge for up to 3 days.

THC
1.3mg per serving;
5.3mg total recipe

Cannabis Leaf Crisps

MUNCHIES TEST KITCHEN
Serves 4

550g/1lb 4oz cannabis fan leaves

1½ teaspoons flower-infused olive oil (see page 64)

Kosher salt or coarse sea salt

Save the kale chips for precious Brooklyn toddlers and chow down on pot-leaf crisps instead. No, they won't get you high on their own (that's what the infused olive oil is for), but it still wouldn't kill you to eat some greens. In fact, it would do you some good. Cannabis, just like all those other leafy greens, is loaded with protein, fibre, vitamins C and K, folate, iron, antioxidants and more.

Heat the oven to 130°C fan/150°C/300°F/gas 2. Line two large baking trays with baking parchment.

Divide the cannabis leaves among the prepared baking trays, drizzle evenly with the infused olive oil and then massage the oil gently into the leaves. Spread the leaves into a single layer and season generously with salt.

Bake the leaves until crispy, about 10 to 12 minutes. Leave them to cool to room temperature before serving. Store in an airtight container at room temperature for up to 3 days.

THC
5.2mg per serving;
62.4mg total

Herb Focaccia

MUNCHIES TEST KITCHEN
Serves 12

185ml/6fl oz/¾ cup hot water
(about 45°C/115°F)

1 x 7g/¼oz packet dried
active yeast

½ teaspoon sugar

230g/8oz/1¾ cups plain flour

Kosher salt or coarse sea salt

6 tablespoons flower-infused
olive oil (see page 64)

5g/⅛oz/½ cup dill leaves

10g/¼oz/½ cup fresh
mint leaves

10g/¼oz/½ cup fresh
parsley leaves

5g/⅛oz/¼ cup fresh
oregano leaves

5g/⅛oz/¼ cup fresh
rosemary leaves

2 garlic cloves, minced

Freshly ground black pepper

Freshly squeezed lemon juice
for seasoning

Cannabis leaves for decorating
(optional)

40g/1½oz/½ cup grated
Parmesan cheese

2 tablespoons sesame seeds

Focaccia is deceptively easy; all you have to do is stir the ingredients together, ignore them for a while, then bake, and you end up with a perfectly bubbly, soft-on-the-inside and lightly-fried-on-the-outside flatbread. This particular version is topped with Parmesan, a ton of fresh herbs and fresh *herb*. It will keep in an airtight container for up to 5 days at room temperature and is especially good with the Homemade Ricotta Cheese on page 233, or dunked in olive oil, either infused or regular.

In the bowl of a food mixer fitted with the dough hook, combine the water, yeast and sugar and leave to sit until foamy, about 10 minutes. Add the flour and ½ teaspoon salt and then mix on medium speed until a smooth dough forms, about 5 minutes. Cover the bowl with cling film and let the dough rise for 30 minutes.

Drizzle 2 tablespoons of the infused olive oil on a 23 by 33-cm/ 9 by 13-inch baking tray.

Once the dough has risen, using your fingers and hands, stretch it into the prepared tray. Stretch and dimple the dough over the course of the next hour to ensure it's the size of the tray (keep it covered with cling film when you're not dimpling it).

In a food processor, combine the dill, mint, parsley, oregano, rosemary and garlic and pulse to mix. Season with 1½ teaspoons salt, 1½ teaspoons pepper and lemon juice, then stream in the remaining 4 tablespoons infused oil until you have a perfect loose paste with which to top your dough.

Top the dough with the herb paste, decorate with cannabis leaves (if using), and sprinkle with the Parmesan, sesame seeds and salt and pepper. Leave to rise for about 45 minutes.

Heat the oven to 200°C fan/220°C/425°F/gas 7.

Using your fingers, gently press dimples into the surface of the dough for the final time, then bake until golden brown, about 20 minutes. Leave to cool slightly, then cut into 12 slices and serve.

THC
8.3mg per roll;
133.6mg total recipe

Dinner Rolls

Timothy Hollingsworth/Otium
Makes 16 rolls

For the Rolls

125ml/4fl oz/½ cup lukewarm water (about 43°C/110°F)

2¼ teaspoons dried active yeast

540g/1lb 3oz/4 cups plain flour

60g/2oz/¼ cup sugar

1½ teaspoons kosher salt or coarse sea salt

125ml/4fl oz/½ cup whole milk

4 tablespoons flower-infused butter (see page 68), melted

1 egg, lightly beaten

2 tablespoons olive oil

For the Egg Wash

2 egg yolks

3 tablespoons water

1 teaspoon kosher salt or coarse sea salt

From chef Timothy Hollingsworth of L.A.'s Otium restaurant come these soft, pillowy dinner rolls ideal for stuffing carbs into your face. Brushing infused butter on these rolls is a hella easy way to add weed to any meal without going to a whole lot of trouble. Leftover rolls will keep in an airtight container, at room temperature, for up to 3 days.

To make the rolls: Put the warm water in the bowl of a food mixer fitted with the dough hook attachment and stir in the yeast. Leave to stand until foamy, about 10 minutes. Meanwhile, in a medium bowl, stir together the flour, sugar and salt.

Add the flour mixture, milk, infused butter and egg to the mixer bowl and beat on low speed for 5 minutes. Increase the speed to medium-high and beat until the dough is smooth and elastic, about 5 minutes longer.

Grease a large bowl with 1 tablespoon of the olive oil. Gather up the dough, shape into a ball, transfer to the oiled bowl and turn the dough to coat all sides with oil. Cover the bowl with cling film and let the dough rise in a warm area until it doubles in size, about 1 hour. Punch the dough down, re-cover the bowl and refrigerate for 1 hour longer.

Grease a 30-cm/12-inch cast-iron frying pan with the remaining 1 tablespoon olive oil. Portion the dough into 16 equal balls and nestle them, not touching, in the pan. Cover loosely with cling film and leave to rise in a warm area until the rolls have doubled in size, about 1 hour.

To make the egg wash: In a small bowl, whisk together the egg yolks, water and salt and set aside.

4 tablespoons flower-infused butter (see page 68), melted

1 tablespoon finely chopped fresh thyme

1 tablespoon crushed Aleppo pepper

1 garlic clove, minced

Grated zest of 1 lemon

Freshly ground black pepper

Maldon sea salt

Vanessa Says: Use a herbaceous, piney strain of weed, like Jack Herer or Romulan, to infuse the butter for these rolls. Up the THC dose (and add a nice shine) by brushing more infused butter on top.

To make the herb butter: In a small bowl, whisk together the infused butter, thyme, Aleppo pepper, garlic and lemon zest and season with black pepper. Set aside.

Heat the oven to 160°C fan/180°C/350°F/gas 4.

Brush the tops of the rolls with the egg wash, then sprinkle each roll with a small pinch of Maldon salt.

Bake the rolls for 20 minutes. Remove the frying pan from the oven and brush the tops of the rolls with all of the herb butter, dividing it evenly. Return the pan to the oven and bake until the rolls are golden brown on top, about 10 minutes longer. Serve warm.

THC
8.4mg per serving;
100mg total recipe

Corn Scones

ZOE TAYLOR/MILKTOOTH
Makes 12 scones

480g/17oz/3⅔ cups plain flour

1 tablespoon kosher salt or coarse sea salt

1 teaspoon bicarbonate of soda

6 tablespoons flower-infused butter (see page 68), frozen and grated on the large holes of a box grater

6 tablespoons unsalted butter, frozen and grated on the large holes of a box grater

185ml/6fl oz/¾ cup buttermilk

185ml/6fl oz/¾ cup soured cream

140g/5oz/1 cup fresh or frozen sweetcorn kernels

At Milktooth in Indianapolis, Zoe Taylor folds grilled sweetcorn kernels into her otherwise super-classic buttermilk scones, which gives them a little sweetness, a little smoke and a little texture. Here, we're amplifying the sweetness with fresh corn (though frozen works too). Zoe's lightly infused cherry elderberry jam (see page 230) makes the scones late-summer appropriate; if it's any other season, the weed-infused honey on page 74 ups the ante nicely. Leftover scones will keep in an airtight container, at room temperature, for up to 5 days.

Heat the oven to 170°C fan/190°C/375°F/gas 5. Line a baking tray with baking parchment and set aside.

In a large bowl, stir together the flour, salt and bicarbonate of soda. Scatter both butters over the top and, using your fingers, mix the butters with the flour mixture just until pea-sized crumbles form. Add the buttermilk and soured cream and mix with your hands just until combined, taking care not to overmix. Stir in the sweetcorn kernels.

Turn the dough out onto a lightly floured work surface. Pat into a large rectangle 2cm/¾ inch thick and then fold over onto itself five or six times (this helps create the flaky layers that we know and love about scones). Pat the dough out again about 2cm/¾ inch thick. Using a 6-cm/2½-inch round biscuit cutter, cut out 12 scones, pressing straight down and pulling straight up to form them. Do not twist the cutter as you lift or you will mess up all those buttery, flaky layers you created by folding the dough over onto itself. As the scones are cut, transfer them to the prepared baking tray, spacing them about 2.5cm/1 inch apart.

Bake the scones until golden brown, about 15 minutes, and rotating the pan 180 degrees halfway through baking. Serve warm.

Preserved Lemons

JOAN NATHAN

Makes 8 lemons

8 lemons, plus 240ml/8fl oz/
1 cup freshly squeezed lemon
juice, or as needed

140g/5oz/1 cup kosher salt or
coarse sea salt

2 grams cannabis flowers, fresh
or dried and cured

2 tablespoons flower-infused
olive oil (see page 64)

Vanessa Says: We threw some
fresh buds in here for fun and
flavour. Pick a variety high in
limonene (such as Super Lemon
Haze) or add some herbaceous
notes with Jack Herer.

Preserved lemons are a North African pantry staple used to brighten
stews, sauces and salads. This version, which includes a couple of
spoonfuls of infused olive oil and some buds, promises to brighten
your day, too. Most of the infused oil will remain in the lemony brine,
which can be repurposed into an ingredient for salad dressing. If
giving as a gift, make the jar decorative by arranging a few fan leaves
around the perimeter.

Wash a large canning jar and lid with hot, soapy water, then sterilise
them by submerging in boiling water for 30 to 60 seconds. Drain
well, transfer to a work surface and leave to air-dry.

Cut a thin slice off both ends of each lemon. Quarter each lemon
lengthways, cutting only three-quarters of the way through, so
the base remains intact. Pack 2 tablespoons of the salt inside each
lemon, pushing the salt into the crevices, and then press the lemon
closed. Pack the stuffed lemons into the sterilised jar, layering in the
cannabis flowers as you go. The lemons should fit snugly in the jar.
Finally, pour in the lemon juice, immersing the lemons in the juice.
Screw on the lid and set the jar aside in a cool place for 1 day.

The next day, add the infused olive oil, recap the jar and then turn
it upside down to distribute the oil evenly. Place the jar in the fridge
and leave to cure for 2 to 3 weeks, until the peels are tender to the
bite. The cured lemons will keep, in the fridge, for up to 3 months.

Rinse the salt from the lemons before using, then scrape off the pulp
(or not if you prefer) and use the peel.

*Note: You can shorten the curing period by about 2 weeks by freezing
the lemons (pack them into a plastic freezer bag) for a few days after you
quarter them. Freezing alters the flesh and peel to speed the penetration of
the salt. Defrost and cure with the salt and other ingredients as directed.*

THC
0.8mg per 2 tablespoons;
39.1mg total recipe

Cherry Elderberry Jam

Zoe Taylor/Milktooth
Makes about 1.8kg/4lb/6½ cups

900g/2lb dark, sweet cherries, stoned and halved (stones reserved)

800g/1lb 12oz/4 cups sugar

2 fresh bay leaves

1 cinnamon stick

1 tablespoon glycerine cannabis tincture (see page 83)

950ml/32fl oz/4 cups elderberry juice

4 tablespoons powdered apple pectin

2 vanilla pods, split lengthways

Kosher salt or coarse sea salt

Freshly squeezed lemon juice for seasoning

This is a low-dose spread for slathering on corn scones (see page 226) but also for dressing up your morning toast or anything else you might like. You will need three 450-ml/16-fl oz/1-pint canning jars with flat lids and screw bands for storing. (Any remaining jam can be kept in a covered container in the fridge.) Wash the jars and lids in hot, soapy water, then sterilise the jars by immersing in gently boiling water for 10 minutes and covering the flat lids with boiling water off the heat. Remove the jars from the boiling water, draining them well, just before you are ready to fill them. Have the lids and screw bands ready.

A well-stocked health food store should have both the elderberry juice and the apple pectin (which helps jam solidify).

In a large saucepan over a medium-low heat, combine the cherries and half the sugar and cook, stirring often to prevent scorching, until the cherries are soft, about 5 minutes. While the cherries cook, put the reserved cherry stones, bay leaves and cinnamon stick on a piece of muslin and tie together the corners to make a sachet.

When the cherries are soft, add the sachet to the pan along with the remaining sugar, the tincture, elderberry juice and pectin. Using the tip of a knife, scrape the seeds from the vanilla pods, then add the seeds and the pods to the pan. Increase the heat to medium-high and bring to the boil. Turn the heat down to a simmer and cook, stirring occasionally, until the mixture is thick and shiny, about 30 minutes. Season with salt and lemon juice.

Place a wire rack in the bottom of a large, tall stockpot, fill the pot three-quarters full of water and bring to the boil.

Ladle the jam into hot, sterilised jars, leaving 5-mm/¼-inch headspace, and wipe away any drips from the rim with a damp towel. Top each jar with a flat lid and twist on a screw band. Using jar tongs, lower the jars into the stockpot. The jars should not be touching one another and should be covered by 2.5cm/1 inch of water. Return the water to a rolling boil, cover and process for 10 minutes. Turn off the heat, leave to cool for a few minutes, then, using tongs, transfer the jars to a rack or a towel-lined work surface and leave to cool completely.

To check if the seal is good on each jar, press against the centre of the lid with a fingertip. If the lid remains concave when you remove your finger, the seal is good; if the lid springs back, the seal failed and the jar must be stored in the fridge. Jars with a good seal can be stored in a cool, dark place for up to 1 year. Once a jar has been opened, store it in the fridge, where it will keep for up to 3 months.

THC
9.2mg per 2 tablespoons;
110.7mg total recipe

Homemade Peanut Butter

Melissa D'Elia
Makes 335g/11¾oz/1½ cups

270g/9½oz/2 cups unsalted raw peanuts

5 tablespoons flower-infused peanut or vegetable oil (see page 64)

60ml/2fl oz/¼ cup whipped weed-infused honey (see page 74)

Kosher salt or coarse sea salt

This pot-laced peanut butter from cannabis chef Melissa D'Elia is amazingly easy and ridiculously good in both sweet and savoury dishes, like the sauce for the Brownie Sundae on page 195 and the Peanut Butter Noodles on page 146, as well as on those nights where all you can manage to make for yourself is a PB&J. Don't be lazy and skip the peanut-roasting step – it gives the finished peanut butter a deeper flavour and smoother texture.

Heat the oven to 160°C fan/180°C/350°F/gas 4.

Spread the peanuts in a single layer on a baking tray and roast until lightly golden and glossy, 7 to 8 minutes. Remove from the oven and leave to cool until just warm.

Transfer the warm peanuts to a food processor and process for 1 minute. Stop the processor and scrape down the sides and along the bottom of the bowl. The peanut butter will be granular and look a bit like wet sand. Repeat the 1-minute processing and scraping four or five times, until the peanut butter begins to look glossy. Drizzle in the infused peanut oil and honey, sprinkle with salt and purée until smooth. Taste and adjust the seasoning if needed.

Transfer the peanut butter to an airtight container and store in the fridge for up to 6 weeks.

THC
4mg per 1 tablespoon;
192mg total recipe

Homemade Ricotta Cheese

FRANK PINELLO/BEST PIZZA

Makes 680g/1lb 8oz/3 cups

1.9 litres/64fl oz whole milk

240ml/8fl oz/1 cup weed-infused cream (see page 72)

½ teaspoon kosher salt or coarse sea salt

3 tablespoons freshly squeezed lemon juice

Owner of Best Pizza in Brooklyn, just a stone's throw from the offices of VICE, and host of *The Pizza Show* on MUNCHIES, Frank Pinello is a friend and a damn fine *pizzaiolo* (a person who makes pizzas), as we can testify from having eaten many a slice. His ricotta is – as expected – killer in the Summer Tomato and Stone Fruit Salad on page 120 or the French Bread Pizza on page 110, but maybe even better with a spoon, on your couch, by yourself.

Line a large strainer with muslin and place over a large bowl.

In a medium saucepan over a medium heat, combine the milk, infused cream and salt and bring just to the boil, stirring constantly to prevent scorching. Turn the heat down to a low simmer, add the lemon juice and cook until the mixture curdles and separates into clumps of milky-white curds and thin ivory whey, about 10 minutes. Remove from the heat.

Slowly pour the contents of the pan into the prepared strainer (it can splash if you work too quickly), leave to drain for 1 hour and then discard the whey.

Transfer the ricotta to an airtight container and store in the fridge for up to 2 days.

THC
10mg per ½ cup;
80mg total recipe

Cannabis Kimchi

Holden Jagger/Altered Plates
Makes about 1.1kg/2lb 7oz

450g/1lb cannabis fan leaves, soaked in water to cover

450g/1lb napa (Chinese leaf) cabbage, cut into 2.5-cm/ 1-inch pieces

50g/1¾oz/¼ cup Korean sea salt

6 garlic cloves, grated

1 tablespoon peeled and grated fresh ginger

1 gram cannabis flower, ground and decarboxylated (see page 54)

3 tablespoons kelp powder

4 tablespoons Korean red pepper powder (gochugaru)

225g/8oz Korean radish (mu) or daikon radish (mooli), peeled and julienned

4 spring onions, white and tender green parts, cut into 5-mm/¼-inch pieces

Cannabis adds subtle dankness to already-funky kimchi. Fresh leaves won't get you high, but they will add THCA to your diet – call it a herbal supplement. The decarb'ed bud is what delivers the potency here, plus it amps up the weed flavour. Holden Jagger is a private chef who grows his own weed and loves experimenting with plant parts. Know that cannabis leaves are deceptively lightweight, so 450g/1lb of them will be more than you might think. After you harvest the leaves, immediately submerge them in water to keep them from wilting. They can be stored this way overnight, either refrigerated or at room temperature. For the Korean-specific ingredients, depending on where you live, visit a Korean market or shop online.

Remove the cannabis leaves from the water and cut them into 1-cm/½-inch slices. If using large fan leaves, feel free to add some of the stem as well; it will add another level of texture.

In a large bowl, mix together the cannabis leaves and cabbage and pour in the salt. With clean or gloved hands, massage the salt into the vegetables until they soften and begin to release their liquid. Cover the bowl and let the mixture sit at room temperature for 2 hours.

Meanwhile, wash a 1-litre/35-fl oz wide-mouthed canning jar and lid with hot, soapy water, then sterilise by submerging them in boiling water for 30 to 60 seconds. Drain well, transfer to a work surface and leave to air-dry.

In a small bowl, combine the garlic, ginger, cannabis flower, kelp powder and red pepper powder and stir to form a paste.

When the 2 hours are up, transfer the cannabis-cabbage mixture to a colander and rinse under cool running water. Squeeze the vegetables, expelling as much liquid as possible. Rinse the large bowl, then return the vegetables to it. Add the radish, spring onions and spice paste, then don gloves and use your hands to mix everything together, working vigorously.

Leaving the gloves on, carefully fill the sterilised jar with the mixture, leaving about 2.5-cm/1-inch headspace. Loosely screw on the sterilised lid. Do *not* tighten the lid, as an airtight seal can create pressure as the kimchi ferments, causing the jar to explode.

Leave the jar in a cool, dry place out of direct sunlight. The jar will release some interesting aromas as it ferments over the next 5 days, but that's part of the magic! After 5 days, the kimchi should be nice and ripe and the jar will have filled with liquid. Tighten the lid and refrigerate for up to 3 months.

Gravadlax

JOSH POLLACK/ROSENBERG'S BAGELS & DELICATESSEN

Makes 800g/1lb 12oz (about 8 servings)

210g/7½oz/1½ cups kosher salt

15g/½oz/1 cup packed fresh dill leaves, plus more for serving

150g/5½oz/¾ cup sugar

2 tablespoons black peppercorns, lightly crushed

1 tablespoon ground mace

Grated zest of 3 lemons, plus 1 lemon, thinly sliced crossways

1 x 900g/2lb piece centre-cut, skin-on salmon fillet (pin bones removed)

3 tablespoons Everclear cannabis tincture (see page 80)

Going viral on the internet is a double-edged sword. Like, maybe, one 420, you post a video of yourself making 'ganja gravlax', the internet loses its mind and the health department shows up at your bagel shop to tell you to knock it off. Not that Josh Pollack, who gave us this salmon recipe that he definitely *doesn't* serve at Rosenberg's Bagels & Delicatessen in Denver, would know anything about that. What he does know, however, is that a few tablespoons of strong Everclear-based weed tincture added during gravadlax making when you would normally add aquavit makes brunch a lot more interesting. This is a three-day waiting game, so plan ahead. Serve this heady gravadlax with bagels and your favourite schmears (spreads) and vegetables.

In a small bowl, stir together the salt, dill leaves, sugar, peppercorns, mace and lemon zest, mixing well.

Lay a double-thick sheet of cling film large enough to wrap the salmon on a work surface.

Place the salmon, skin-side down, on the centre of the cling film. Season the flesh side evenly with the salt mixture, then sprinkle evenly with the tincture. Wrap the salmon tightly in the film and place, flesh-side down, in a baking dish. Refrigerate for 48 hours.

Remove the baking dish from the fridge, flip the salmon and gently massage it, still wrapped, to redistribute the brine. Return to the fridge to cure for 24 hours longer. When fully cured, the gravadlax will be firm to the touch at the thickest part.

Set a wire rack in a baking tray or have ready a clean baking dish.

Unwrap the salmon, discarding any excess brine. Rinse the fish lightly under cool running water and pat dry with paper towels. Place the salmon, skin-side down, on the rack or in the dish and refrigerate, uncovered, overnight.

Cut the salmon against the grain into paper-thin slices to serve.

Pot Pepperoni

JUSTIN SEVERINO

Makes 2.7kg/6lb

4.5kg/10lb boneless
pork shoulder

4g/⅛oz Bactoferm F-RM-52
meat starter culture

125ml/4fl oz/½ cup tepid water

70g/2½oz/½ cup kosher salt or
coarse sea salt

50g/1¾oz/¼ cup sugar

25g/1oz/¼ cup smoked paprika

2 teaspoons cayenne pepper

1 tablespoon fennel seeds

1½ teaspoons curing salt #2
(aka Prague Powder #2)

1 teaspoon ground allspice

6 tablespoons red wine

5 tablespoons Everclear
cannabis tincture (see page 80)

9m/30 feet x 40mm/1½ inches
hog casings, rinsed to remove
salt, then soaked in room-
temperature water for 45 to
60 minutes, until pliable

Pittsburgh chef and whole-animal butcher Justin Severino knows his way around meat – and isn't unfamiliar with cannabis either. We tasked him with coming up with a way to combine the two, and this pot-laced pepperoni is the result. Sure, it's ambitious. But it's also amazing. Drop slices on the French Bread Pizza on page 110, or set it out with a plate of the Homemade Ricotta Cheese on page 233 for the kind of cheese-and-charcuterie platter stoner dreams are made of.

Cut the pork into 2–2.5-cm/¾–1-inch pieces, pile it into a big container, and put it in the freezer until firm but not frozen, about 30 minutes.

Meanwhile, set up your meat grinder and fit it with the medium die plate.

Pass half of the chilled meat through the grinder, capturing it in a large bowl. Switch out the medium die for the fine die and pass the remaining meat through the grinder, capturing it in the same bowl.

In a small plastic container, dissolve the starter culture in the water and leave to stand for 5 minutes.

Meanwhile, add the kosher salt, sugar, paprika, cayenne, fennel seeds, curing salt, allspice, wine and tincture to the pork and, using your hands, mix until all of the ingredients are evenly distributed. Transfer the sausage to a food mixer fitted with the paddle attachment. On low speed, add the starter culture solution in a thin stream and continue to mix until the mixture becomes tacky and starts to stick to the sides of the bowl.

Set up your sausage stuffer. Moisten the nozzle of the stuffer with water and slide the casings onto the nozzle. Turn on the stuffer and press some of the meat into the stuffer hopper until about 2.5cm/1 inch of meat protrudes from the tip. Turn off the machine, pull some of the casing from the nozzle over the meat and tie a knot

continued

at the tip, taking care to press out any air pockets. You can use a pin or cake tester to poke any small holes in the casing to release air. Turn the machine back on and gently press the meat through the stuffer and into the casing, coiling the sausage on your work surface as you go, until you have used up all of the meat.

Cut off any excess casing, pressing out air pockets, and tie a knot at the end. To form the filled casing into links, starting at a tied end, measure off two 30-cm/12-inch lengths, then twist about four times in one direction between the first and second lengths and twist about four times in the opposite direction after the second length. Repeat until you have a chain of 30-cm/12-inch-long sausages.

Tie the sausages into loops and load them onto wooden rods on a drying rack. Ferment at 38°C/100°F and 100 per cent humidity for 12 hours, until the sausages have a pH reading of 4.5 to 5.0. Transfer them to a drying chamber and age at 13°C/55°F and 60 per cent humidity for 4 weeks, until the pepperoni have lost 30 per cent of their original weight or have reached an AW (water activity) reading of 0.84.

Refrigerate the pepperoni for up to 3 months.

THC
10mg per patty/link;
150mg total recipe

Hot or Sweet Italian Sausage

CARA NICOLETTI

Makes 15 x 150g/5½oz patties or links

2.25kg/5lb minced pork shoulder, very cold

For the Hot Sausage

35g/1¼oz/¼ cup kosher salt

35g/1¼oz/⅓ cup smoked paprika

4 garlic cloves, mashed to a paste

2 tablespoons fennel seeds, toasted; two-thirds ground to a powder and one-third left whole

4 teaspoons chilli flakes

2 teaspoons cayenne pepper

1½ teaspoons sugar

1 teaspoon freshly ground black pepper

1 teaspoon coriander seeds

1.9 grams cannabis flower, ground and decarboxylated (see page 54)

60ml/2fl oz/¼ cup red wine, chilled

If we were going to ask anyone to show us how to make weed sausage, it had to be Cara Nicoletti, a fourth-generation butcher and baker (and host of MUNCHIES' *Hangover Show*) whose Instagram is basically a shiny rainbow of sausage. Sausage making takes practice to get right – your own personal sausage Instagram might have to delay its launch until you perfect your sausage skills – but it's worth it. Where else are you going to find sausage that gets you high?

Place the pork in the bowl of a food mixer fitted with the paddle attachment. Turn the mixer to its lowest speed.

To make the hot sausage: Add the salt, paprika, garlic, fennel seeds, chilli flakes, cayenne, sugar, black pepper, coriander seeds and cannabis flower to the mixer and mix for exactly 1½ minutes (set a timer!). Add the wine and mix for exactly 1½ minutes. The mixture is now ready to shape into patties or links.

To make the sweet sausage: Add the salt, garlic, fennel seeds, sugar, black pepper and cannabis flower to the mixer and mix for exactly 1 minute (set a timer!). Add the parsley and rosemary and mix for exactly 1 minute longer. Finally, add the wine and mix for exactly 1 minute. The mixture is now ready to shape into patties or links.

To form sausage patties, divide the mixture into 15 portions and flatten into disks about 2cm/¾ inch thick. To store in the fridge, stack the patties, separating them with squares of baking parchment, then slip into ziplock bags or other airtight containers and refrigerate for up to 5 days. To store in the freezer, arrange the patties in a single layer on baking parchment–lined baking trays, place in the freezer until frozen, then transfer to ziplock freezer bags and return to the freezer for up to 3 months.

continued

Hot or Sweet Italian Sausage, *continued*

For the Sweet Sausage

35g/1¼oz/¼ cup kosher salt

3 garlic cloves, mashed to a paste

2 tablespoons fennel seeds, toasted; two-thirds ground to a powder and one-third left whole

1½ teaspoons sugar

1 teaspoon freshly ground black pepper

1.9 grams cannabis flower, ground and decarboxylated (see page 54)

Leaves from 1 large bunch flat-leaf parsley, finely chopped

Leaves from 4 rosemary sprigs, finely chopped

125ml/4fl oz/½ cup dry white wine, chilled

2.5m/8 feet x 32–36-mm/ 1¼–1½-inch hog casings, rinsed to remove salt, then soaked in room-temperature water for 45 to 60 minutes, until pliable

To form sausage links, set up your sausage stuffer. Moisten the nozzle of the stuffer with water and slide the casings onto the nozzle. Turn on the stuffer and press some of the meat into the stuffer hopper until about 2.5cm/1 inch of meat protrudes from the tip. Turn off the machine, pull some of the casing from the nozzle over the meat, and tie a knot at the tip, taking care to press out any air pockets. You can use a pin or cake tester to poke any small holes in the casing to release air. Turn the machine back on and gently press the meat through the stuffer and into the casing, creating 1.2-m/4-foot lengths. Cut off any excess casing, pressing out air pockets, and tie a knot at the end. Coil the sausage on your work surface as you go, until you have used up all of the meat.

Starting at one tied end, pinch the filled casing into 13-cm/5-inch lengths, twisting each link a few times in one direction at each pinch. Poke them all over with a pin or cocktail stick and refrigerate overnight, uncovered, before cooking. To store in the fridge, transfer to a ziplock bag in a single layer and refrigerate for up to 5 days. To store in the freezer, arrange the sausages in a single layer on baking parchment-lined baking trays, place in the freezer until frozen, then transfer to ziplock freezer bags and freeze for up to 3 months.

When ready to cook, heat the oven to 160°C fan/180°C/350°F/ gas 4. Place the sausages on a baking tray and bake until golden and a thermometer inserted reaches 70°C/160°F, about 17 to 20 minutes.

THC
10mg per patty/link;
180mg total recipe

Broccoli Rabe and Provolone Sausage

Cara Nicoletti

Makes 18 x 150g/5½oz patties or links

450g/1lb broccoli rabe (rapini or turnip tops), tough stem ends discarded

2.25kg/5lb minced pork shoulder, very cold

35g/1¼oz/¼ cup kosher salt

7 garlic cloves, mashed to a paste

Grated zest of 1 lemon

4 teaspoons chilli flakes

1 tablespoon sugar

1 teaspoon freshly ground black pepper

2.8 grams cannabis flower, ground and decarboxylated (see page 54)

1 tablespoon red wine vinegar

60ml/2fl oz/¼ cup ice-cold water

450g/1lb provolone cheese, cut into 5-mm/¼-inch cubes

2.75m/9 feet x 32–36-mm/ 1¼–1½-inch hog casings, rinsed to remove salt, then soaked in room-temperature water for 45 to 60 minutes, until pliable

These cheesy green sausages are especially good grilled and served with a side of peppers and onions. The cheese makes them particularly juicy, so beware when biting in.

Bring a medium saucepan of water to the boil. Meanwhile, fill a large bowl with water and ice.

When the water is boiling, add the broccoli rabe and cook, uncovered, until tender, about 5 minutes. Drain the broccoli rabe and plunge it into the iced water to stop the cooking. Once it has cooled, drain well, then squeeze thoroughly to remove any water.

Transfer the broccoli rabe to a food processor and process until it is almost paste-like. (You can add a little olive oil to the processor if needed for the blade to move freely.)

Place the pork in the bowl of a food mixer fitted with the paddle attachment. Turn the mixer to its lowest speed, add the salt, garlic and lemon zest, and mix for 10 seconds. Add the chilli flakes, sugar, black pepper and cannabis flower and mix for exactly 1 minute (set a timer!). Add the broccoli rabe and mix for exactly 1 minute longer. Stir the vinegar into the ice-cold water, add to the mixture and mix for exactly 30 seconds. Add the cheese and mix for exactly 30 seconds longer. The mixture is now ready to shape into patties or links.

To form sausage patties, divide the mixture into 18 portions and flatten into disks about 2cm/¾ inch thick. To store in the fridge, stack the patties, separating them with squares of baking parchment, then slip into ziplock bags or other airtight containers and refrigerate for up to 5 days. To store in the freezer, arrange the patties in a single layer on parchment-lined baking trays, place in the freezer until frozen, then transfer to ziplock freezer bags and freeze for up to 3 months.

To form sausage links, set up your sausage stuffer. Moisten the nozzle of the stuffer with water and slide the casings onto the nozzle. Turn on the stuffer and press some of the meat into the stuffer hopper until about 2.5cm/1 inch of meat protrudes from the tip. Turn off the machine, pull some of the casing from the nozzle over the meat, and tie a knot at the tip, taking care to press out any air pockets. You can use a pin or cake tester to poke any small holes in the casing to release air. Turn the machine back on and gently press the meat through the stuffer and into the casing, creating 1.2-m/4-foot lengths. Cut off any excess casing, pressing out air pockets, and tie a knot at the end. Coil the sausage on your work surface as you go, until you have used up all of the meat.

Starting at one tied end, pinch the filled casing into 13-cm/5-inch lengths, twisting each link a few times in one direction at each pinch. Poke them all over with a pin or cocktail stick and refrigerate overnight, uncovered, before cooking. To store in the fridge, transfer to a ziplock bag in a single layer and refrigerate for up to 5 days. To store in the freezer, arrange the sausages in a single layer on parchment-lined baking trays, place in the freezer until frozen, then transfer to ziplock freezer bags and freeze for up to 3 months.

When ready to cook, heat the oven to 160°C fan/180°C/350°F/ gas 4. Place the sausages on a baking tray and bake until golden and a thermometer inserted reaches 70°C/160°F, about 17 to 20 minutes.

Resources

What you'll be able to get depends, of course, on where you live. But assuming you have some choice in the matter, we've listed a couple of suggestions for how to pair the strains you're most likely to come across as well as some of our favourite providers.

Ry's Pairing Suggestions for Popular Strains

AK-47 • Piney, fruity, sharp • Has a pungent herbal component similar to rosemary; great for chicken.

Blue Dream • Floral, herbal, sweet • This herb-forward varietal is soft enough to use in desserts, but also works well in light, savoury dishes.

Bubba Kush • Earthy, sweet, rich • One of the richest-tasting varieties around; its leathery chocolate funk has Scotch-like qualities.

Chemdog • Sharp, funky, gassy • The acridity makes it difficult to pair with most food, but it's good for cutting through fatty foods or adding deep flavour to drinks.

Cookies • Sweet, earthy, rich • Similar chocolate and coffee notes to Gorilla Glue, but sweeter and less obtrusive.

Dosidos • Earthy, sweet, floral • Its sweet, hashy, chocolate-kissed qualities do well in not-too-sweet desserts.

Gorilla Glue • Rich, earthy, gassy • Works well in chocolate desserts or in richer savoury dishes.

Green Crack • Tangy, sweet, fruity • A versatile variety with lots of fruity notes; adds a great aromatic component to cocktails and works really well in desserts.

Maui Wowie • Piney, floral, earthy • Works well across most courses.

OG Kush • Sharp, earthy, gassy • Works well with stronger flavours – think coffee, or savoury mains like short ribs or lamb.

Purple Urkle • Sweet, floral, fruity • Complex and extremely fragrant, best used for lighter dishes where its uniqueness can shine through.

Sour Diesel • Sharp, bright, gassy • Not quite as acrid and savoury as its sister strain Chemdog; it's brighter and plays nicely with fish and chicken.

Strawberry Banana • Fruity, creamy, sweet • Has a delicate, distinct strawberry-banana-smoothie flavour and would work well in something neutral, like cheesecake.

Super Lemon Haze • Sweet, creamy, fruity • Distinct-tasting but lighter, and good for desserts and drinks.

Super Silver Haze • Bright, herbal, floral • Often carries lemongrass and eucalyptus qualities, which go super-well with Thai curry.

Tangie • Citrusy, tangy, floral • An excellent aromatic; adds an incredible, almost-uncanny citrus punch to drinks and sauces.

Acknowledgements

Special thanks to the writer of this book, Elise McDonough, for her off- and on-set assistance. Her cannabis knowledge and styling skills, plus her endless supply of weed puns, were invaluable throughout the project. A big thank-you to our publisher, Ten Speed Press, and the dedicated editorial team guiding this project: editor Emily Timberlake, Doug Ogan, Serena Sigona, Carey Jones, designer Kara Plikaitis and Sharon Silva. As well as the entire staff at Ten Speed, especially Aaron Wehner, Maya Mavjee, Hannah Rahill, Windy Dorresteyn, David Hawk, Daniel Wikey and Allison Renzulli.

A very special thanks to producer Jason Pinsky, and *Bong Appétit* cast members Vanessa Lavorato and Ry Prichard; first for how their creativity and knowledge has expanded the boundaries of what we know about cannabis cuisine, and also for their extensive help on this book.

Thanks to MUNCHIES publisher John Martin, channel manager Tommy Lucente, Nyasha Shani Foy and Leslie Stern for their continuous support in our printed efforts. Thanks so much to *Bong Appétit* executive producers Lauren Cynamon and Chris Grosso, co-executive producer Ari Fishman, and the entire cast and crew of *Bong Appétit* involved in making the MUNCHIES Digital and VICELAND series: Gayle Gilman, Erica Winograd, Tracy Wares, David Bienenstock, Elana Schulman, Peter Courtien, Abdullah Saeed, Jason Pinsky, Tami Alfasi, Ariel Algus, Jessica Bahr, Kathleen Flood, Talin Middleton, Carrie Cheek, Allie Stefan, Davina Dobrovech, Armen Karapetian, Hunter Johnson, JonPaul Douglas, Kyle Marchant, Travis Wood, Ronnie Silva, Lex Sadasivan, Alex Wills, Lex Sadasivan, Genéa Gaudet, Ronnie Silva, David Croom, Adam Daroff, Meryl Goodwin, Marley Lister, Katherine Bernard, Arkie Tadesse, Joshua Argue, Will Nails, Zachary Rockwood, Kazmo Kida, Jen White, Ryan Sak, Joeshua Wright, Andre Evans, Robbie Renfrow, Shane Tilston, Sunny Sawhney, George Olivo, Austin Higgins, Karlos Miguel, Dee Wasielewska and Kalid Hussein.

Thank you to our friends at FremantleMedia, especially Keith Hindle and Elena Magula, and the Tiny Riot team: Regina Leckel, Devon Dunlap, Jessica Porper and Nathan Rea.

Thank you so much to our agents at the Gernert Company: Anna Worrall, Chris Parris-Lamb, David Gernert and Paula Breen.

Thanks so much to photographer Marcus Nilsson and world-class photo assistant and hand model, Peter Baker. WE LOVE LA! WE LOVE IT! Thank you to illustrator Ho-Mui Wong for creating beautiful, instructional images that will prevent people from sending themselves to hospital.

A special thanks to the cutting-edge science used by cannabis lab The Werc Shop and Dr. Jeffrey Raber for helping us understand the test results and efficiency of THC infusions. Science is a powerful drug.

Thanks to marijuana grower Kyle Kushman for providing the marijuana strains Forbidden Fruit, Candyland and Starberry, and Platinum GSC cannabis and Veganic kief for the recipe testing and photography in the book. Thanks to Addison DeMoura and Alex 'Poof' from Rezn Extracts, for providing high-end hash and also a Mothership. Special thanks to Purple Frost Genetics for the pre-rolls and flowers, and Kenny Morrow for commenting on the significance of terpenes and extraction technology.

Thanks to our prop stylist, Amy Chin, and her incredible assistant, Lux Wright. Thank you to our recipe testers, Yewande Komolafe and Julie Beth Tanous – we will never look at flies or shortbread cookies the same way ever again. A big thanks to our kitchen interns Andrew Richmond, Justin Ayoub, Widza Gustin and Alex Burris for helping us during this cookbook process. Special thanks to Yolande Mabiko for truly helping us make this book in ways we could never imagine.

A huge thanks to our dear friend Khuong Phan. Special thanks to Ariel Stark-Benz of Mister Green for providing so many of the beautiful props in this book, along with Little Garage Shop, Stonedware, Concrete Cat and Group Partner.

None of this would have been possible without the participation of the chefs and collaborators featured, including Aurora Leveroni, Barbara Leung, Bryant Terry, Cara Nicoletti, Chris Lanter, Christine Ha, Courtney McBroom, Dan Nelson, Daniela Soto-Innes, David Posey, David Wilcox, Deuki Hong, Devon Tarby, Don Lee, Erika Nakamura, Fatima Ali, Frank Pinello, Holden Jagger, Iliana Regan, Jasmine Shimoda, Joan Nathan, Jocelyn Guest, John Clark, Jonathan Brooks, Josh Pollack, Justin Severino, Kelly Fields, Louis Tikaram, Mason Hereford, Melissa D'Elia, Melissa Fernandez, Michelle Gayer, Mindy Segal, Natalia Pereira, Rebecca Merhej, Sam Smith, Sarah Kramer, Sheldon Simeon, Thu Tran, Tim Milojevich, Timothy Hollingsworth, Tracy Obolsky, Yoya Takahashi and Zoe Taylor.

Additional thanks to Colleen Cleary and Joey Lozada at OXO, Barry Frish, Omar Midence, Jason Favreau, Daniel Bonomo and David DiNoble.

Thanks to VICE co-founders Shane Smith and Suroosh Alvi, co-presidents Andrew Creighton and James Schwab, and the entire VICE team.

The MUNCHIES team would like to thank our former editor in chief, Helen Hollyman, for all her work on this cookbook and art direction on the photo shoot. Thank you to our culinary director, Farideh Sadeghin, for spearheading the recipes in this book, managing our team of recipe testers and styling the beautiful food; while our editor in chief, Rupa Bhattacharya, smoothed out all the edges and herded all the cats. Massive thanks and gratitude to the entire MUNCHIES family around the globe, and especially our inimitable senior editor Hilary Pollack and wonderful social editor Sydney Mondry, for holding down the fort while we got this book done, as well as staff writer Mayukh Sen and editorial assistant Danielle Wayda, for tolerating endless weed conversations in Slack.

#420blazeit

Index

In parts of the United Kingdom and in many other countries, it is a criminal offence to cultivate, possess or supply cannabis. As these offences can carry heavy penalties, such as imprisonment and/or fines, you should research your local laws. This book's purpose is private entertainment and is not intended to encourage the disobedience of any law.

First published in the United Kingdom in 2018 by
Pavilion
An imprint of HarperCollins*Publishers* Ltd
1 London Bridge Street
London SE1 9GF

www.harpercollins.co.uk

HarperCollins*Publishers*
Macken House,
39/40 Mayor Street Upper
Dublin 1,
D01 C9W8,
Ireland

ISBN 978-1-911624-56-1

A CIP catalogue record for this book is available from the British Library.

10 9 8 7

Printed and bound by Papercraft, Malaysia

www.pavilionbooks.com

First published in the United States by Ten Speed Press, an imprint of the Crown Publishing Group, a division of Penguin Random House LLC, New York.

www.crownpublishing.com
www.tenspeed.com

Ten Speed Press and the Ten Speed Press colophon are registered trademarks of Penguin Random House LLC.

MIX
Paper | Supporting responsible forestry
FSC™ C007454

This book is produced from independently certified FSC™ paper to ensure responsible forest management.

For more information visit: www.harpercollins.co.uk/green